Better Lucky Than Clever

Better Lucky Than Clever

Maurice Hussey

Better Lucky Than Clever
by Maurice Hussey

Produced and published in 2015 by Briar Press

A catalogue card for this book is
available from the British Library

ISBN: 9780993485800

Cover image: Author's library
(1930, Crossways - Author and Gingie)

Publication managed by TJ INK
tjink.co.uk

Printed and bound by TJ International, Cornwall, UK

For Becca, without whom this book would probably never have been started and certainly would not have been finished.

Contents

CHAPTER 1

Downside 1942–1947

Totting up my brushes with death so far, a Hurricane crashing into a school cricket match and killing nine boys is probably the one closest to an actual hit.

I went to Downside in September 1942 when I was thirteen and a half. It was on the Mendips about fifteen miles from Bath, and was attached to the monastery which, in turn, was dominated by the Abbey Church.

As an institution it was large and intimidating and, with about two hundred boys, far bigger than my prep school. The abbey tower dominated the countryside and was a landmark for miles around.

Unlike my prep school, which had been evacuated to a village surrounded by all the bomber command airfields of East Anglia and my home near Reading, where I had seen a dogfight with lots of vapour trails and the (possibly imaginary) sound of machine guns, Downside seemed a long way from the war.

What literally sought us out were the Hurricane fighter pilots being trained at Yeovil. They used our playing fields to practise hedge hopping. We rather enjoyed seeing them and it was certainly spectacular as they flew well below tree top height; it normally didn't last very long.

One Saturday in May 1943, the school were watching the first eleven playing a cricket match, sitting as usual on the long bank with the pavilion in the middle, which divided the first eleven pitch from the all the others. The bank was about seven or eight feet high with a lower ledge about four feet from the top.

I was playing in an under-fifteen match in the upper field, about fifty yards away from where the school were sitting.

That afternoon we saw two Hurricanes arrive as they flew east to west over the school and across the first eleven pitch about fifty feet up; the instructor was in the leading plane and the idea was for the novice in the second aircraft to follow him. Quite suddenly we heard the second pilot in trouble; there were some trees at the west end of the ground and maybe he turned too tight to try and avoid them, possibly even clipping one in the process. He lost flying speed and what we heard, and then saw, was his desperate response, revving the engine to try and avoid stalling. The sound of a Merlin engine on full power heading straight towards you is not easily forgotten. He had responded far too late.

A Hurricane was not large as military aircraft go. Close up, it looked huge as it passed about thirty yards away from us and twenty feet up, then hit the ground and bounced along the bank where the boys were sitting. The pilot ejected from the plane, but his parachute got caught in the cockpit and swung him round breaking his neck. He might have survived had he stayed in the cockpit, which finished up more or less intact resting against the pavilion. Suddenly it was quiet; it had all lasted barely a minute. Then the Hurricane caught fire and the ammunition started to explode, adding the smell of cordite to the smell of the crash.

We survivors went towards the crashed plane to try and help but were shooed away and eventually made our way down to the school; most of the injured required specialist treatment which was obviously beyond us.

We discovered later that in addition to the pilot nine boys had been killed and about the same number injured. Viewed in the abstract this seems surprisingly few and must have been due to the majority of the boys sitting on the lower ledge of the bank; in addition I believe there were instances of the plane actually bouncing over boys lying on the ground.

There was a queue for the telephone to tell our families we had been lucky. It had been reported on the radio as 'a Catholic school in the west country' which was good enough for my mother – by the time I phoned she was nearly incapable of speech.

I imagine nowadays we would receive professional counselling; I doubt if anyone had heard of it then. As it was, the following day was Sunday and there were in any case no lessons and by Monday we were back to normal routine.

Gradually, after some months, some of the injured came back into school and I became friendly with a boy who had been badly burned. He had taken up making tiny and exquisite models of aeroplanes out of matchsticks, beautifully finished and mounted in boxes made of Perspex. This fed two of my obsessions, aeroplanes and modelling, so I bought some from him. I think he had instinctively found his own form of therapy.

Not much changed after the crash. The Air Force promised they wouldn't do it again. As for the instructor pilot (he was an old boy of the school), I doubt if anything very serious happened to him. In 1943 trained pilots were not going to be sacrificed for doing something foolish and dangerous.

I hadn't been in the school long enough to get to know many other boys; the first year boys were in any case somewhat segregated, kept in what was called the 'junior house,' so before the accident I didn't know any of those killed or injured.

Round about this time at a farm not far from my parents a couple of locals had stopped for a chat; they had finished their business and moved on. Shortly afterwards a German bomber making for home jettisoned its last bomb and left a crater where they had been standing. They had been lucky.

By contrast the boys watching the cricket had been unlucky. All over England at that stage in the war some people were getting killed, while others were fortunate. So we didn't discuss the crash – there didn't seem a lot of point. It was just down to luck, some of it excruciating.

On the evening of the tragedy, there was a roll-call. Everyone was accounted for except for a boy called Bidwell in the lower sixth. I don't think any great panic ensued because he was definitely not the sort to watch cricket matches. Eventually he turned up and after some fairly high-powered interrogation admitted that he had been doing what he always did on Saturday afternoons, namely driving one of the steam trains on the 'Slow and Dirty' otherwise the Somerset and Dorset Railway, from our local station Chilcompton down to Poole and back. The drivers were delighted to run an ad hoc apprenticeship scheme and Bidwell fulfilled what was well known to be every boy's dream – driving a steam engine. The arrangement terminated abruptly.

Bidwell moved on to more intellectual devilment, latching on to The Church Times. Like the rest of us indoctrinated Catholics, he tended to hold Anglican theology in some contempt and decided to launch an extremely recondite (and absurd) theological debate in its correspondence pages, between the Reverend Athelstan Lattie and the Reverend Gurney Smeed (both clergymen being Bidwell in disguise, of course). After several months of intensive theological research and composition, the Church Times got wise to it and called a halt.

There was a further venture which also came to a sudden end, involving the headmastership of a totally imaginary public school. The final episode was when Bidwell sent out an invitation to all the headmasters he could think of, to some self-evidently idiotic conference. I believe the take-up rate was quite low but worth the effort for the reply from the headmaster of Winchester, who claimed to be attending a seminar on celibacy in Salt Lake City. Bidwell would have loved to have thought of that.

There was a rumour that the RAF had banned low flying near the school and we were to report any planes we saw. This was an invitation to the robuster elements every now and then to make a concerted rush to the window 'to report a low flying aircraft sir' This made life purgatory for some of less effective masters such as the junior French master.

The senior French master was a different matter. Called M. Cartel he was a musical comedy Frenchman, short and stout with an imperial beard and a small dour wife. He was a ferocious disciplinarian. At home he brought with him a little bit of France in the form of a primitive sauna. This was a wooden box about four foot square which he sat in with his head sticking out of a hole in the top while he gently steamed. The legend was that on one occasion the heating arrangement had malfunctioned and he was half-way to being cooked before Mme Cartel heard his screams and released him. No one was brave enough to question him about it.

A lot of the teaching was done by monks and generally they taught very well. In fact I think we preferred them to the masters. From the parents' point of view, I suppose that, as the monks came free, so to speak, it appeared that the school was short-changing the parents unless there was a sprinkling of lay staff. The circumstances of war meant that occasionally we would get someone who was very odd indeed.

There were six or seven of us in the upper sixth classics set and we were being taught by the headmaster who clearly wanted to be shot of us. One day Granville Conway appeared. He was slim, well inside call-up age, wearing a repellent mustard coloured check suit and a brown silk handkerchief flopping out of his breast pocket. The headmaster had been the leading classics scholar of his year at Cambridge; Granville clearly had not. In fact by the end of the morning we had marked him down as a complete poser – that was the polite version. Even his name was dubious, it sounded as though it had been filched from a novel by Trollope.

The setting of homework was the acid test; he set an absurd amount, clearly without any idea of what he was doing. A deputation was sent to the headmaster and Granville did not reappear.

Funnily enough he did re-appear about five years later when I was at Oxford, still wearing the mustard coloured suit or its cousin. He told me, quite without embarrassment that he was reading for a pass degree in Classics. I never saw him again, certainly not at lectures.

Most of the monks who taught us were lovely men who regarded us as an opportunity to practise Christian Resignation. One was Father Ralph, known as 'Tusker' on account of his prominent buck teeth. He was prone to blushing and a good opening gambit was for one of the more innocent looking members of the class to say "Please sir, can you tell us the difference between a helot and a harlot?" This was guaranteed to send him purple with embarrassment but there was a definite limit to how often it could be employed. Contrast and compare, as they say the headmaster dealing with the problem of Sappho, "Sappho was a lady, that is to say a member of the female sex." We knew where we stood with Sappho but we never found out about the helot and the harlot – as though we didn't know. Father Ralph was a brilliant teacher. He took me for school certificate (GCSE) English and I enjoyed every minute. I can still remember chunks of Twelfth Night and, more improbably, some of the poems of Thomas Gray, which were our two set books.

Father Lucius known for some reason as 'Buzzy' was another teacher who was a considerable character. Quite short, with a fringe of grey hair, he was very erudite but subject to a clearly obsessional urge to prove that almost any character from history you chose to name was actually at heart a Catholic. There were limits, but the game was to see how far one makes him go. Thus Charles the Second was a doddle, Oliver Cromwell perhaps a step too far. Meanwhile it provided instant relaxation from the rigours of whatever subject he was supposed to be teaching.

The other characteristic of Father Lucius was his susceptibility to thunderstorms, not just unease but total collapse. A particularly violent one occurred during one of his lessons and he rushed out pale and shaking. One of the class, showing more responsibility than we usually did, went after him to his room in the monastery. After negotiating all the piles of books littering the floor, he found him under the bed and comforted him till the storm was over.

A monk whom I do not recollect doing any teaching, though he ran the JTC, was Father Cuthbert. He had won the Military Cross during the First World War and had remained in the Guards when it ended. There was a piece in the New Statesman 'This England' column quoting from the Times "In 1923 he gave up a gilded career and retired to the monastery at Downside, retaining only his membership of the Guards Club". History didn't relate how often he used it. The club was founded as a boating club at Maidenhead for Guards officers in the nineteenth century but later achieved a somewhat raffish reputation, mainly on account of its Ascot and Regatta balls. I suppose that, by virtue of having strictly no accommodation for women, it could be said to have accorded in part with monastic tradition.

As Downside was primarily a monastery with a school attached, a certain amount of our time was spent in the abbey church. Plainsong suited my entirely unformed musical tastes and the austerity of the abbey set off the robes and incense of the ceremony. On major feasts of the church, we would have a pontifical high mass when the Abbot in full robes and mitre, carrying his crozier, would process down the abbey. When they reached the choir, the Abbot would enter his stall and the attendant deacons and sub-deacons would carry on to the sanctuary.

My housemaster at the time owned a Staffordshire Bull Terrier called Grock. He was a lovely dog and a great favourite with all the boys. However Grock's sex life was something of a public scandal and he flaunted his private parts in a way that was definitely un-monastic. On the occasion I have in mind, my housemaster was taking part in the service and Grock thought he might tag along. The choir processed down the aisle and, greatly to everyone's delight, there was Grock waggling his balls, closely following the abbot, looking like some mediaeval allegory of sin lurking in the shadow of religious observance. They reached the choir and the abbot went to his stall. I should mention that the abbot was well over six foot tall with an aquiline aristocratic nose and a formidable presence. The abbot turned round and saw Grock. Nothing was said. The abbot looked at Grock. Grock looked the abbot. Grock suddenly let out a wild howl as though he had been exorcised and shot out of the abbey. We all felt it was a most edifying addition to the service.

The procession was headed by the Thurifer, the acolyte in charge of the thurible in which the incense was smouldering. The post was a coveted one among the senior boys; you had to be tall and have a dignified demeanour. The thurible was made of silver and weighed five or six pounds and the idea was to keep it swinging regularly on a four foot chain so that the incense was kept burning and giving off its fragrance without banging into anything and wrecking it. The climax of the whole performance was the point where the Thurifer, leading the procession out of the sanctuary, had to make a sharp left turn just in front of where the junior boys were sitting; the trick was to see how close to them you could get the thurible at head height, without their screaming or actually beaning them.

There was a fundamental problem with the abbey. Fuel was scarce and I suspect using it to heat such a large building, which in any case was used only intermittently, was deemed unpatriotic. So a compromise was reached and only those radiators towards the front of the church, where the school sat, were heated. The result was spectacular. Convection currents, worthy of a wind-tunnel or the original pentecostal blast, circulated round the building, the hot air from the radiators rising straight to the roof of the nave and then circulating round the building before returning to the congregation in refrigerant form.

When Easter fell early enough to be incorporated into the spring term we would take part in the Holy Week rituals. Whatever one's feelings or the strength of one's beliefs, they were undeniably something of a challenge. The grand-daddy of them all was Maundy Thursday, four hours solid before breakfast. I found them incredibly moving and though I had absolutely no idea of it at the time, they probably prepared me for long nights at Wagner's operas. Parsifal is easy going for someone who has cut his teeth on Maundy Thursday.

Life at Downside was pretty civilised. I probably made the worst of it by being games obsessive and when not actually playing or worrying about whether games were going to be rained off (frequently) or merely lose (also fairly frequently), I tended to spend my time in the library. I was a persistent reader and the library was a great place to do it. In addition to being one of the few places where the central heating really worked, there was an open coal fire in cold weather. A set of alcoves with tables stretched down one side and it was warm and distraction free. Also there was a huge collection of books. A strict and rather eccentric censorship applied, mainly to do with sex, but tempered by age and reputation; so Shakespeare and even Congreve or Wycherley were okay, while Greene and Waugh were suspect. My taste was quite unformed so that today I am as surprised by what I did read as much as what I didn't; a huge amount of Shakespeare in fact, but also most of Marlowe and a lot of Kipling and Chesterton. How did I come to choose?

Saturday afternoons were free if you weren't playing games, which I generally was, and a lot of ingenuity was used in finding somewhere safe to smoke. As it happened I never felt any urge to do this, but there was a period when I had some free Saturdays and my friend Miles who was good organist persuaded me to go on organ playing expeditions with him. We used to cycle to various small Mendip churches; they were normally open and I pumped while he played. We had no permission from anyone and the Vicar would generally appear, all set to be indignant. Fortunately Miles had a lot of charm as well as being a good organist so we never got into trouble, although, being pathologically law-abiding, I used to go into agonies of apprehension each time we started to play. It didn't last very long. After a bit I decided I was definitely on the wrong end of the deal, pumping the organ was hard work; but looking back I take a lot of pleasure in remembering the time spent cycling on empty roads through lovely countryside to beautiful churches that were open to anyone.

Below the sixth form we used to do 'prep' in the evening in the Gasquet Hall. A pleasant source of distraction was the huge collection of stuffed animal heads. These covered the walls of the hall and also stretched down the main corridors. They were all buck or herbivores of one kind or another; there were no lion and since it was all African, tigers didn't come into it.The biggest was the head and neck of an African buffalo, injudiciously placed over the doorway to the 'Junior House' where new boys spent their first year in the school. I remember ducking in and out as fast as possible under it. It did eventually come down – quite a spectacular event in itself and no one was killed. One peculiarity was that whereas the bigger animals came with full head and neck, a lot of the smaller ones had only a bare head or even antlers only. Meditating during prep, I came to the manifestly absurd conclusion that they gradually shrank and disappeared into the wooden plaque on which they were mounted. I never did work out what the logic of it was.

Something else to look at were the rows of rugger and cricket team photographs. Although I played for two successive years in the rugger first fifteen I never made it into the photo because by the time it came to be taken they had always discovered how useless I was.

Cricket was better; I was in two of the photographs and nearly made it into a third when I was under sixteen. The older pictures were far more fun. The rugger teams from the early nineteen hundreds all looked as though they were about twenty-five with luxuriant moustaches. Despite this their rugger caps – purely ornamental with lots of red velvet, gold braid and tassels – gave them a surprisingly effeminate air.

CHAPTER 1

Although it had nothing to do with Downside, something happened in 1946, my fourth year in the school, which certainly contributed to my education. I think my father realised that my parents' rather claustrophobic life style, partly due to war time restrictions, but also to his disinclination ever to leave the farm, contributed a lot to my mother's now chronic ill-health.

The remedy he lit on was for my mother to take me on a holiday to Switzerland. My parents had lived there very happily for nearly four years, when they were first married and I had been born there. There may have been further motive. The surgeon, who had operated on my father eighteen years before, was still around, probably in his late fifties or early sixties. It was a good opportunity to show our gratitude.

On the other hand it must be remembered that this was ten years before a continental holiday became regarded as an Englishman's birth right, moreover there were still millions of people throughout Europe who were displaced and homeless. So it was a fairly dashing decision. My only previous holiday had been a fortnight in Deal, eight years before, which I hadn't enjoyed much. I was far from enthusiastic, mainly on the idiotic grounds that summer was the time for playing cricket, and possibly because I hadn't got used to the idea that the war was properly over. Apart from being born there, I had never actually been 'abroad'.

At the end of the war, my father calculated he had made a net loss of fifty pounds from the chickens during the whole period of the war, so cash was a problem. He had however built up a collection of Swiss stamps. My personal view was that of all hobbies, stamp collecting was the most boring and, of all stamps, Swiss stamps were also the most boring. There was some evidence for this as they all had the same picture of a lady, looking rather like Britannia, but actually representing Helvetia which came in various shades of sludge green. I, rather self-centredly, saw no reason for not disposing of some of these. My father probably saw it rather differently. Anyway this was to provide the financial backing for the trip. We also purchased Travellers Cheques. There were strict limits on the amount one could take out of the country so we took the maximum.

Come the great day and we set out for London with a decent wodge of stamps concealed under drawer lining paper in my mother's suitcase. She seemed entirely happy with the arrangement, I wasn't so sure; but then I hadn't got her taste for criminality.

We spent a miserable night in a shared room at the Grosvenor Hotel at Victoria; an endless series of hoots and whistles and clanks and groans. Down to Dover in the morning, time to discover I wasn't a good sailor (why wasn't I at home playing cricket?) and there was the train waiting to take us to Switzerland. The journey was interminable; could it have taken thirty-six hours? The view of France from the train was shocking. I had been spared the sight of blitzed cities in England and the country-side at home was mostly untouched. This was country that had been fought over and destroyed. Even our picnic showed the effect of wartime – our bottle of wine certainly did. It wasn't a happy journey.

It must have been the following morning that we reached Lucerne. We had booked into an hotel but the agent told us that it had been found to be unsatisfactory – there was talk of drains - so we had been transferred to one of the best hotels for the same money. After six years of austerity - not a lot to eat, no heating, no petrol, trains not working - we were suddenly plunged into a land of milk and honey and could hardly believe how lucky we were to be enjoying it. For their part, the Swiss had suffered from the absence of tourists during the war and were desperately keen to get them back, particularly the British who had always been good customers and who, having won the war, presumably had more money than the rest of the Europeans. Not these Brits as it happened.

One way of showing their desire to re-open tourists links was to offer a rate of exchange on travellers cheques roughly double the open market rate. So we took our full allowance of travellers' cheques and then made an excursion to Berne to see Zumstein, the Stanley Gibbons of Switzerland. The policy of client confidentiality clearly extended not merely to banks but also to stamp dealers and the inscrutable dealers at Zumstein showed no surprise at my mother grubbing around in her suitcase and emerging with quite a valuable collection of Swiss stamps. The deal was done and we emerged with lots of Swiss francs which we distributed round our pockets; although it seemed almost indecent to contemplate being robbed in such a well-ordered city as Berne.

Lucerne was incredible. We rowed on the lake, walked on the old bridge with the Dance of Death pictures, sat by the lake and ate cream cakes. One in particular looked like a fish cake. My mother encouraged me "You'll really like it" -I really did. There was a memorable moment at our posh hotel. At dinner one evening, a disturbance centred round two elderly ladies dressed in what could have passed for Salvation Army uniform. My mother whispered "I think they may be drunk, dear." She was right.They were absolutely slaughtered. I hadn't come across this before and it certainly livened things up.

I loved Switzerland. It brought out all my most bourgeois instincts and tastes. I loved the wooden chalets with the logs piled neatly up under the eaves ready for the orderly white snow which would be falling in a few months. I loved the spick and span farms and the cattle with their cow-bells. I loved the trains, running on time and going surprisingly quickly over the passes and through the long twisty tunnels. We took a coach trip over the Furka and Grimsel passes, notable for a Yorkshire lady who discovered she had no head for heights and spent the whole trip weeping quietly on the floor of the bus.

We went up the Jungfraujoch and later took a train to Lugano. This was strange as when we came out of the tunnel, the air changed from being cool and crisp to being warm and balmy. The Swiss orderliness and cleanliness had also vanished in the tunnel. This was Italy or if it wasn't, it was the next best thing.

I could have taken dual Swiss nationality; the deal-breaker was doing two lots of military service.

It was time to come home.There was one last thing to do; to visit a currency exchange to cash our travellers cheques and then, after a decent interval, sell back the francs at the open market rate. It was a significant amount and my mother cashed it into fifty pound notes and hid it in her knitting wool. "Darling, no one would dare to unravel all that wool" – and she was quite right.

Another long train journey, confirmation that I was definitely not a good sailor, back to Henley and home. It was a memorable trip.

I was very nearly killed on my last morning at Downside. My parents had come down to help me collect the bits and bobs from my study so I was still around the morning after the end of term. The staff were busy collecting all the bedding from the dormitories and just as I stepped out of the doorway of the house I was in, they dropped a bag with about fifty sets of bedding from two floors up; it probably weighed fifty pounds and just brushed me as it fell. It was a curious farewell.

My mother and me, school holidays 1943

CHAPTER 2

My father's family 1895–1927

I was now seventeen and the rule 'pas devant les enfants' had been subtly relaxed so that over the past year or two, I had been gradually getting to know some of the family history. On my father's side of the family it had been fairly exciting.

To go back quite a long way, my father's mother known to me as 'Granny' had gone to Ireland in 1895 to marry my grandfather Maurice Fitzgerald Hussey. My mother always claimed it was an arranged marriage. It might well have been something like that and his reputation could well have appealed to my grandmother. He was notably good-looking, an extremely skilful rider, had a good business and at that time was living in Loughglynn House, a huge Georgian ansion overlooking the Lough, which he leased from his friend Viscount Dillon.

In due course my grandparents had two children: my father Maurice Henry Murray, known as 'Bill', and John Edward or 'Jack.' My grandparents were part of a racing set; Granny's sister married a prominent racehorse trainer called Peter Purcell Gilpin who at that time lived not far away and the families became close.

Like his father, Samuel Murray, my grandfather's principal occupation was as a land agent for some big estates and, in the years after 1895, this had gradually come to a halt with compulsory purchases of these estates by the government. In the meanwhile, he had acquired some expensive habits, notably owning race horses (he was well capable of riding them himself) and drinking too much. On top of this, there were several attempts to kill him; someone nicknamed him 'snipe' because he was so difficult to shoot. There was an occasion when he was warned not to accompany his wife and children back from the races and they were actually stopped by an armed gang who only let them go when they discovered he wasn't in the carriage.

Granny even carried a pistol herself. It was tiny, very pretty, with a mother of pearl handle and firing .22 pellets. I confiscated it from her in her eighties, the risk to her from Sinn Fein having by then somewhat diminished. This atmosphere of violence did nothing for marital harmony and Granny had a constitutional incompatibility with the Irish. Or perhaps, she may simply have found it too stressful to be continually a target for shooting.

Jack was born in 1902 and at some point after this, I surmise about 1903 or 1904, Granny walked out, taking the two boys to England. No one had much to say about this period although there are a number of photographs of my father in front of various stately homes where the boys and their mother had been staying after their departure to England. It was clearly very distressing at a time when divorce and even separation could lead to social ostracism, although in her case, it seems not to have occurred. Perhaps it was recognised in English society that living in South West Ireland at the time required talents which not everyone shared. She and my grandfather were never divorced.

I have three letters relating to this period which shed light on my grandfather's situation. The first is from Viscount Dillon and is clearly intended as a reference for my grandfather as a land agent to show to a future employer. He mentions the fact that the Dillon estate in Ireland has been compulsorily purchased, the implication being that my grandfather had lost his main source of income. The next is an offer from Lord Dunraven of a job as stud manager at Adare Manor. It is dated 1914, two years before my grandfather died at the age of fifty eight. Reading it is an interesting exercise in social niceties from long ago. It begins "My dear Mr Hussey"; the 'my' is somewhat condescending, especially taken with the 'Mr.' A social equal would get 'Dear Hussey' , a friend 'My dear Hussey' and a prospective butler 'Mr Hussey'. It is signed off 'yours truly' which is what the butler would get. My grandfather was after all a JP and a considerable landowner himself so I don't suppose he was very impressed with the letter. The salary was £400, say £20000 today. There were no travelling expenses and the job was a hundred miles away from home so it sounds as though it might either have been kindly meant or, more likely, as a cheap offer which he couldn't afford to refuse. There is no record of his accepting.

The final letter is from my father to his mother, written while he was on holiday in Ireland and is dated August 1909 so my father was just turned thirteen. The interesting thing about this letter is that my father talks about the gamekeeper and so on but there is not a word about his own father. Maybe this just reflects the extreme acrimony then existing between my grandparents, so that he was reluctant to mention his father in a letter to his mother, or perhaps it was because my grandfather couldn't cope with the youngster. My father mentioned once to me that at dinner the butler would produce his employer's medicine and then would always have to take some first to get my grandfather to take it. This all suggests someone in considerable decline.

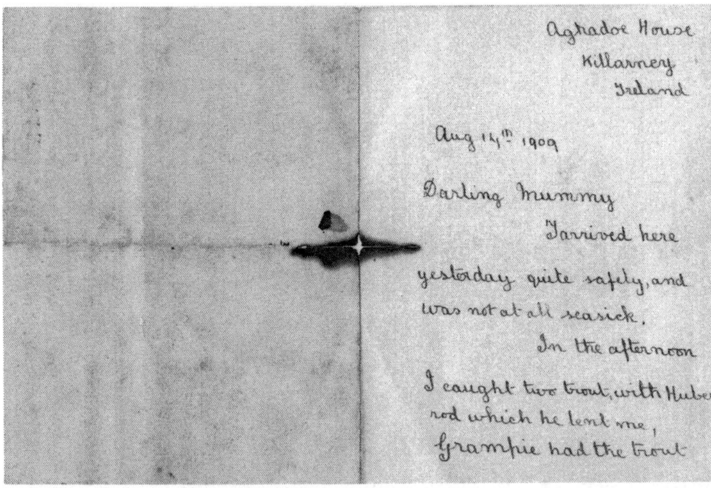

Aghadoe House
Killarney
Ireland

Aug 14th 1909

Darling Mummy

I arrived here yesterday quite safely, and was not at all seasick.

In the afternoon I caught two trout, with Hubert's rod which he lent me, Grampie had the trout

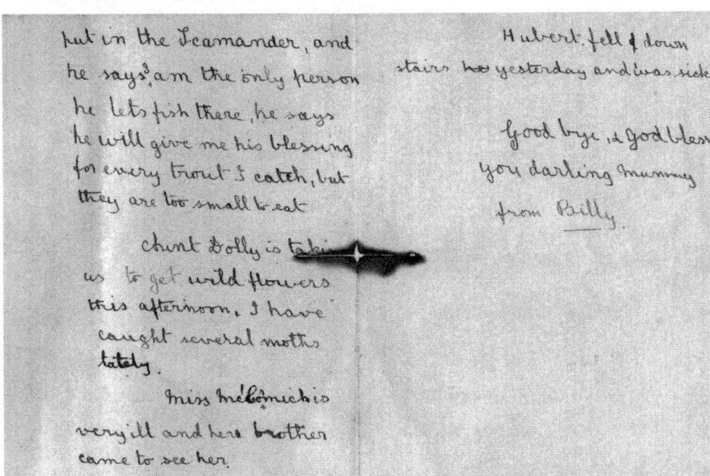

put in the Scamander, and he says I am the only person he lets fish there, he says he will give me his blessing for every trout I catch, but they are too small to eat

Aunt Dolly is taking us to get wild flowers this afternoon. I have caught several moths lately.

Miss McCormick is very ill and hers brother came to see her.

Hubert fell down stairs yesterday and was sick.

Good bye, & God bless you darling Mummy

from Billy

Meanwhile Granny was living in England with the two boys as a wealthy socialite. I know absolutely nothing about this period in her life. The one recollection my father passed on, was that as a teenager, he helped his mother with her corsets by putting his knee in the small of her back and tugging at the strings. I suppose her wasp waist in the photos is more a tribute to his strength than to her figure.

Oh and there was a story Granny told me herself, relating to the war years, when she got a friend's cook – a foreign national – arrested as a spy. Total warfare.

Eight years after the war, and my uncle Jack had come back from America, where he had worked as a stock broker in the big boom of the twenties with not a lot to show for it except a serious drink problem. The traditional remedy for younger sons who had 'blotted their copy book' was to ship them out to the colonies and Jack was duly despatched to Southern Rhodesia (Zimbabwe) to work on a cousin's farm. This finished after a couple of years when he shot himself in the foot. The comic side of this disappears completely in real life, particularly when the weapon is a shot gun. Jack's leg was amputated below the knee and for the rest of his life he was seriously crippled, as shot-gun pellets kept working out of his leg giving him considerable pain and discomfort.

I really know very little about my father's life during this period. He was eighteen at the outbreak of war and must have been excused service on the grounds of having TB. I know he taught for a time, but he never spoke much about this part of his life. By 1927 I know he was a neighbour of my mother's family in Great Mongeham in Kent.

It was about this time that my parents met and quite quickly got engaged. This must have been a dreadful period in Granny's life. Separated from her husband, then widowed, her elder son was seriously ill with TB, was about to marry a Catholic and had become a Catholic himself. In the process his relations with her had been broken off, or at least severely damaged, while her younger son had acquired a drink problem and had crippled himself into the bargain.

Granny was bitterly opposed to my parents marrying and I have one of her letters to my mother which is savage. There is a puzzle surrounding it. It is something of scrawl and barely legible and my mother told me that it had never actually been sent; but how then did she get hold of it? Even though they became reconciled maybe four or five years later, I can't believe that that extended to swapping drafts of letters awash with such venom.

Reading it again the other day, I noticed that according to Granny my parents had only met three weeks before they were going to get married. If that were true it would put a rather different complexion on the matter. I should have thought there would have been huge opposition from both sides of the family. There is a rather plaintive letter from 'Gingie,' my mother's mother, who had clearly been saddled with organising a wedding reception that the Borgias might have relished, saying that it had to be at a hotel, because the removal men were due to clear her house the following day. Desperate measures.

One thing which makes me doubtful of the truth of Granny's 'three week' assertion is that my father had been given a course of instruction as a Catholic convert and this in itself would normally have taken at least several months. But then that might well have been organised well before he met my mother.

In passing, he always told me he was much entertained by the instruction he received on 'sins reserved for the bishop.' Far from being some particularly recondite deviancy, it turned out to be mainly restricted to the sin of murder in Southern Ireland where some of the parish priests were far from being capable of being dispassionate confessors. His grandfather had in fact defended a long action for slander brought by a local priest on the grounds that my great grandfather had accused him, by implication, of 'incitement to murder.' I have toiled through the newspaper reports to try and work out what went on. Crucial to the whole case were relations between Father O'Donoghue (the priest involved) and the Macroom Farmers Club. As their avowed policy was the murder of all landlords and tenants, described as 'ridding the land of tyrants,' it sounds as though they didn't require a lot of incitement, but perhaps also were inappropriate associates for the clergy. Then there was the evidence of the Arch Deacon who had had a run-in with Father O'Donoghue previously. It was partly quotations from his letters which were complained of in the writ.

On clear instructions from the judge, the jury fund in favour of the priest with damages assessed at one farthing. So a draw then.

It's easy to feel that my mother must have been out of her mind to contemplate marriage in the circumstances of my father's health. At the time, the prognosis for someone with TB was exceptionally poor. A patient like my father with one seriously infected lung, was probably going to die and was never likely to make a full recovery. And as Granny pointed out, they would not have much money and there wasn't much likelihood of either of them earning even small amounts. And of course living with someone infected with TB brought its own particular risks.

My mother, 'Sis' to the family, always had a will of iron and she had had a tough war as a junior nurse (aged about nineteen) at a hospital in Southend, accepting batches, up to a hundred at a time, of badly injured men from the front. This was sometimes on her own without other help. At night there were Zeppelin raids which caused significant casualties. After about two years, she called a halt – the war was coming to an end anyway – but in one of her letters written towards the end of the war, she talked of going to work in a hospital for incurables. I have sometimes wondered whether marrying my father might have been a substitute for that, although the letter was written a long time before they met, which didn't happen until about eight years after the war. Whatever her reasons, conscious or unconscious, she carried it off. They were married in 1927 and lived happily ever after.

Except that I don't suppose it seemed like that at the time. I know they had some kind of reception – Granny stayed away which was just as well; Jack was there but with his damaged leg, hardly contributing much jollity. There was no driving off into the sunset. Instead it was a case of waiting patiently at Dover for a crossing calm enough for my father to be able to cope.

The Swiss had specialised in the treatment of TB. It was believed at the time that the pure mountain air restricted the spread of the infection within the lung and Swiss surgeons had developed an operation which, provided one lung remained uninfected, offered a hope of a cure by closing down the infected lung.

An appointment had been made with the surgeon for my father to have the operation and they had rented a chalet in Montana, as it was then called, for an indefinite period. This was a small village about five thousand feet up, overlooking the Rhone Valley.

The journey was a problem. It was impossible to do it in one go, and the difficulty was finding a hotel in which to break the journey. There was no disguising the fact of my father being an invalid and hotels showed great reluctance, actually complete refusal, to accept a guest who might be regarded as infectious, unexpectedly delay his departure, or worse still, upset the other the other guests by dying.

My mother found a solution in an advertisement for an establishment which positively welcomed guests with health problems and she signed up for a short stay. It turned out to be rather unusual - most of the inmates were clinically insane. Apart from making socialising difficult, there was the problem that the doors to the rooms could not be opened from the inside. My mother claimed that on one occasion she had heard shouts from one of the rooms of "Madame Houssaie, Madame Housssaie" and had been required to release one of the doctors who had got trapped inside - according to my mother, with a homicidal lunatic - she was never one to let slip a good story. The rest of their journey went according to plan.

The operation which my father had signed up for was pretty heroic. It involved removing all the ribs on one side of the chest and closing down the infected lung. I believe it was only tried in cases that were regarded as terminal and the success rate wasn't high. When the time came for the operation, he was waiting on a trolley when a nurse poked her head round the door and asked what he was having done? "Thoracoplastic," he replied.

"Ah, tous les thoracoplastiques sont malhereusement morts," she said and disappeared again.

Despite this setback my father survived the operation; there is a photograph, which my mother absolutely hated, of him holding his surplus ribs in his mouth like tusks. They spent three years happily living in Montana, my father pottering about and taking photographs, my mother able to go skating (even my father managed this) and skiing when she wasn't looking after my father. Her family came out to stay and there are a number of happy family snaps.

My father, grandfather and great grandfather c 1900

My father and me, 1929

I was born 6th February 1929 and christened Maurice Walter. These were family names; about half my Irish ancestors were called Maurice. But it did so happen that the star players of the Ashes tour of Australia, taking place at the date I was born, were Maurice Tate (fast bowler) and Walter Hammond (star Batsman). Twenty years later when I had got to understand his obsession with cricket, I suggested to my father that my naming wasn't entirely coincidental. He said it was.

CHAPTER 3

Crossways 1930–1947

As it happened I had had another escape about ten or twelve years before the plane crash. When my parents returned from Switzerland in 1930, they bought a house called Crossways near Henley-on-Thames.

Three or so years after settling in to the neighbourhood, my mother had started behaving in an eccentric way. Not that her behaviour was intrinsically odd, but it was seriously out of character. For some reason she had decided that she was going to embark on formal tea-parties with the neighbours and with this in view had signed up a village girl to act as parlour-maid wearing the proper outfit – starched lace and so on. I distinctly remember the outfit; I conclude it must have represented something well out of the ordinary even to a four-year-old.

Who the neighbours were, that she was going to have tea with, remained a mystery. I do remember a succession of these parlour-maids and increasing desperation on my mother's part. None of them had the least idea what was required of them. Looking after me came into the job description and I probably contributed to the rapid turnover by my behaviour.

I can well remember reflecting on my good fortune in being born British and having about a third of the globe coloured pink to signify our empire. I remember wondering what it was like to be born French, say, and having practically no empire at all. I seem to have been able to overlook huge areas of land in Africa and the Far East. I also seem to have skipped the bit about our own starving work force in the north.

God knows how I came by all this – my father was a dedicated socialist and certainly wouldn't have put up with it.

Whatever the reason, I don't think I got on with any of the girls very well and there were frequent complaints. Up to a point my mother put up with this, but one girl definitely went too far by trying to murder me. Suddenly one morning I became aware she was trying to push me out of an upstairs window.

It wasn't a long drop but would certainly have hurt a lot and I didn't want to find out how much; so I resisted violently – a lot of kicking and probably biting – but it was just as well my mother turned up. I suppose we had made quite a lot of noise by then. What my mother made of it I don't know; the girl must have been at least slightly deranged. It certainly brought the succession of housemaids to an abrupt halt which, as far as I was concerned, was definitely a good thing.

In any case, a few years later the war completely put a stop to all this; no more tea-parties and certainly no more parlour-maids. Except that is, for the arrival of Mary O'Connor.

As a good Catholic, my mother was approached by one of the local priests to give Mary a home. She had no known relations or friends, was an albino with a pink complexion and long white hair, normally tied in a bun but reaching down to her waist when combed out. It was not clear how much she could see; her eyes wandered all over the place and she was tiny – under five foot tall. She was supposed to be able to help with housework and also to be a trained cook, but there wasn't much evidence for either of these. On the plus side she wasn't expected to live very long, but no one liked to dwell on that aspect of the matter; it would have seemed callous. Meanwhile she had a ferocious temper and was jealously protective of my mother.

Mary occupied the kitchen, which because of the Aga was the only warm room in the house. My father and I didn't dare go in there, particularly on Sunday mornings which were devoted to reading of the News of the World and doing the 'Spot the Ball' competition. Unsurprisingly, she never got this right and it didn't improve her temper. She lived for more than eleven years with us without any signs of mellowing. All-in-all it was one of the stranger employer/employee relationships.

My father owned two acres of land and, during the war, we took on neighbouring plots to cultivate in the cause of 'digging for victory.' As a consequence, we took on some labour to help. A lady called Dolly Franklin, known to me as Queenie, had been with us for some years and continued right through the war. If ever questioned about her work she used to say "I keep steady on" and there really wasn't any need to question it, as without moving very fast, she got through a lot of work. She lived in a cottage two or three miles away which had an earthen floor and for which she paid half-a-crown (12.5p) rent a week. She never got ill and was entirely content; in fact the only time I knew her get at all upset, was, when she fell off her bike in icy weather, the policeman who found her smelt her breath.

The other long term employee was a gypsy called King – never any second name – who helped my father with the chicken farm. He and I viewed each other with mistrust, mainly because neither could make out what the other was talking about, though in King's case, this was not an unusual situation. He had a range of country skills which included catching and killing mice with his bare hands, and climbing big trees without any harness, lopping and pruning as required. There was an unfortunate incident when he accidentally caught one of our neighbour's cats in a snare. No great harm was done to the cat, but the neighbour, though he would greatly have liked to have a go at my father (whose chicken farm, he thought, lowered the tone of the neighbourhood), was not prepared to tackle King.

Then we had Arthur for a time. He was resident in the local asylum and was incredibly strong, capable of picking up a heavy steel barrow full of rubbish and emptying it at arm's length over the tip. He was very gentle and scared stiff of Alfred (also from the asylum) who worked further up the lane and used to bully him. To get Arthur home, we had to mount a watch on the lane and only release him when Alfred was safely past. It didn't take much to send Arthur into a paroxysm of indecision and on one occasion, when my mother had fallen off some steps and broken her arm, Arthur was the only person around and was so upset that he was completely incapable of getting help.

I lived in the hope that Ethelred might turn out to be the next one on the list but that never happened. For a time a girl called Enid Boggis came to work for us. She was smart and presentable and knew about gardening. She lived in a cottage with her mother who was extremely eccentric. There were also five Alsatians who used to sleep on the beds with them. On one occasion Enid had to make a trip into Reading to go shopping for a larger bed, as one of the dogs had bitten her in the night in a dispute over space. It took some explaining to the assistant.

On another occasion, Enid was returning home in the dusk and saw in the distance a figure about the size of a dog, which turned out to be her mother on all fours (it was very icy) sliding forward like a caterpillar on two mats, off to post a letter. Enid died quite suddenly while I was away at school, much mourned.

During the school holidays I was co-opted into the labour force. My father had seen an advertisement for a 'motorised plough.' This was roughly the shape of an ordinary horse drawn plough but in between the wheels was a powerful two-stroke petrol engine. The problem with it was that with the plough-share in the ground, the engine was at the limit of its capacity and had to be kept running flat out to keep it going at all. With the plough-share out of the ground, of course it went off like a rocket. Moreover the clutch was operated with the right hand so that, when engaging it, one was left holding the plough with the left hand only.

My father had arranged for a demonstration which happened while I was away at school, so I only heard about it later. The salesman did a short bit of ploughing (I think he probably picked his ground carefully) and then invited my father to have a go. With only one lung, he was hardly strong enough to control it. He let in the clutch with the plough skimming across the ground and took out a young pear tree. For some reason this satisfied him and he put in an order.

The plough was undoubtedly the work of the devil. Essentially one had to choose between starting with the plough-share out of the ground, in which case it would take off and, like as not, disappear over the horizon. Or you would start with the plough below ground level and it would stall. So you would start again. My heart had never been in digging for victory and spending the afternoon, wrestling with this beast, did nothing to change it.

A more satisfactory way of spending the afternoon was accompanying my mother driving round on Women's Land Army business. She was in charge of the whole of South Oxfordshire, responsible for placing girls to work on the farms and keeping them happy and in order whilst they were there. She had had some experience of this at the end of the First World War and from her background, knew how to take on the farmers who tended to be grumpy and sometimes devious.

The nature of the girls' situation gave a lot of scope for mayhem of one kind or another. My mother did once say rather moodily that her girls seemed to have a bad effect on stockmen; possibly it was just proximity, although being shut up with someone in a milking parlour at five in the morning can hardly rate high as an erotically charged situation. Many of the problems arose simply because the girls tended to come from urban backgrounds and were completely ignorant of country life and customs. Inevitably they had been pitched into situations where the trained labour had been taken off to war, so there was no one left to train them. For many farmers, they were part of the problem rather than the solution. Anyway there was a lot for my mother and I to do and it helped to keep me away from my nemesis the plough.

We had an American field hospital near us, built on one of the commons. They were a friendly bunch and we used to get visits fairly often. The colonel called on my father for help with finding a horse for one of the orderlies to ride; none too easy at that stage of the war when horses tended to be either working or dead. It seemed an odd request but it appeared that the orderly's father owned most of the pigs in Chicago so the request carried a certain amount of clout. In the interest of British/American solidarity a horse was found for him.

Two of the nurses visited regularly. One was rather small and pugnacious and was always trying to get me to box with her. It used to scare me stiff, but I could never decide in my own mind whether it was fear of hurting her or fear of being humiliated myself that worried me so much, or whether it just offended my sense of what was right. At all events, I managed to get out of it and on the plus side acquired a pair of surplus American army boots, which were supremely inelegant but very well made and comfortable.

My mother was drawn into the war effort. I don't know how he found out, maybe she volunteered the information, but the colonel in charge of the hospital knew that my mother had gone to school in Germany, a convent in Mainz to be precise, just before the First World War I think she spent about two years there and in fact only got out in the nick of time, rescued by her father a couple of days before the outbreak of the first world war. Because she couldn't speak German, the nuns had put her to help in the kitchen – it sounds a rather cynical arrangement – to learn German from the cooks. Apart from being thoroughly provincial, what she learnt was a million miles from 'High German.' Throughout her life my mother took full advantage of this.

The American hospital was used entirely to treat German

prisoners of war, much to the annoyance of the staff. They didn't see any reason why the POW's shouldn't provide useful information, so now my mother was wheeled out to offer tea and sympathy to the German troops in the language, and accent, they felt at home with. I don't know how much information she managed to obtain but she certainly enjoyed herself in her role as official interrogator.

There were some odd people living in our village. One couple interested me as a child although it was a long time before anyone told me any of the details. Their names were Miss Howell and Miss Beatty. Miss Beatty was a large coarse woman, not much liked. Miss Howell on the other hand was small, cultivated and charming, aged about fifty. Nowadays I suppose one would imagine they were a couple but it wasn't actually the case. I used to be taken round to call on Miss Howell and I always enjoyed it. But she had a weakness; at the full moon she was prone to stripping off all her clothes and screaming obscenities; hence the presence of Miss Beatty.

We always referred to 'the village' but it wasn't really a village. The clue was in the names of the places making up the area: Peppard Common, Kingwood Common, Sonning Common. There never had been a proper village - no church, no rectory, not even a village hall. In mediaeval times it must have consisted of areas of common land where villages, some way away, held the grazing rights. These villages had disappeared, with the exception of Sonning, a pretty village down on the Thames and five or six miles from Sonning Common, which in relation to Sonning was something of a cuckoo.

The ground in the area was fairly terrible for any kind of cultivation, so there was little competition to farm it. In the circumstances, its gradual conversion into a dormitory for Reading was probably inevitable. My mother charted its progress.

"You know the house they have just called 'the Manor House'? It used to be a pub called 'the Blue Monkey.".

After the war our chicken farm came under pressure from the neighbours; it was regarded as lowering the tone even though it had been there at least ten years before most of the new arrivals. It was quite true that the area was changing and eventually my father had to surrender the chickens; by then age and ill-health were playing a part. I'm sure the social stresses kept him going longer than he should have done.

He had always been an active Labour Party supporter. At one election the only polling station was located in Henley. It was true that we were nearer to Henley than Reading, five miles as against seven, and the constituency was based in Henley, but there were buses to Reading and none at all to Henley. By and large, Labour supporters didn't have cars so they had no means of getting to vote. Looking back, this seems outrageous and my father and several others were fired up to run a shuttle service to the polling station.

Some of the 'comrades' were fun. There was one, Sid Bishop, who lived mainly by poaching. His weapon of choice was a catapult – he could reliably kill a rabbit at thirty yards with it and it was more or less silent. Then there was a family who ran a small shop, mainly fizzy drinks and sweets. Their ambition was to diversify into ice cream and to do this they needed to steal a freezer from the local TB sanatorium. This wasn't a smash and grab affair but showed considerable patience, one of the lads nicking parts from the freezer they had targeted, until eventually the sanatorium surrendered and sold them the remaining part as scrap.

My father had bought Crossways at auction. Even in the depths of the Great Depression, £1100 for a five bedroom house with two acres of land was not expensive. One day, a year or so after we moved in, a girl who was working for her said to my mother, "This is where he hanged hisself."

This was incorrect as well as being shocking. The wife of the previous owner had been an invalid, permanently bed-ridden and her husband had been totally at her call. He had gradually become unbalanced himself, spent the time hammering nails into all the exposed beams in the house. Finally he purchased a razor and cut his throat.

Early riding ambitions, 1933

One of my father's many photos, 1934

Crossways

My father had not seen fit to mention all this to my mother, so it came as something of a shock. Nevertheless she coped perfectly well and we lived there happily for over thirty years, although it took right to the end of the war to get rid of all the nails.

Shortly after we bought Crossways, my mother's mother (Gingie) rented a small Regency villa about three miles away and I used to go and stay there occasionally. It's difficult to visualise today how little life had changed in the first hundred years or so since it had been built. There was no mains electricity - I don't think it arrived until about 1938 - so at dusk there was the ritual of lighting the oil lamps. Then there was the question of bringing in fuel for the fires - there was of course no central heating - and coal for the cooker. At night and in winter the house was basically cold and dark. You could just about read by the oil lamps. In fact, the principal difference in lifestyle between the early nineteenth century and the twentieth was that now there were few or no servants to help with these tasks. Apart from this, it could have been a scene straight out of Cranford.

At Crossways on the other hand, my father remedied the electricity problem by installing a generator in one of the outhouses. It was large, driven by a diesel engine via a highly dangerous belt and pulley and produced modest amounts of current – just about enough for lighting, certainly no heat. Even so, it would sometimes peter out and my father would have to grab a torch and rush out into the night to persuade it to restart. We got central heating installed not long before the war. This had huge cast-iron radiators which gave out a moderate amount of heat and a lot of noise. It was judged to be certainly a Great Leap Forward.

The telephone arrived sometime before the war. The local exchange was Rotherfield Greys. Our number was 7. The exchange was run by an old duck who also ran the village shop. To make a call, one rang the exchange and asked for the number you needed. Sometimes there was a delay in the exchange responding, and eventually, when they did, there would be the sound of panting, "Sorry dear, I was down the bottom of the garden." After a year or so it all expanded; our number became 71 then 271. Eventually the personal touch vanished altogether and automation took over, losing for ever the option of asking whether Mrs So and So was at home; our exchange was good on that sort of information.

This progressive move into the twentieth century was not mirrored at Gingie's villa. She gave up the tenancy and built herself a house on part of our land. As a family, the Edwardes were actively antipathetic towards anything with pretensions to good design – this house was straight out of the builder's pattern book and was pretty horrid. My father tried to take a hand but gave up in frustration.

In 1930 my uncle Walter bought a farm called Whitcalls about three miles up the road from us, presumably with help from his mother. There was a family excursion to see it and I was taken with them. I can't have been very old, maybe two or three at the most, as I was taken round for a ride on his black Labrador without too much protest from the dog.

We made several visits and went all round the farm. There were some greenhouses with tomatoes and a big wooden barn. The downstairs loo was outside the farmhouse and adjoining a field where his cart-horse Boxer lived. Boxer was friendly and inquisitive, so anyone using the loo was liable to have Boxer suddenly snuffling down the back of their neck. There was a cherry orchard across the lane and some ducks. It was completely idyllic but I remember my father was never very enthusiastic; he could recognise a hopeless proposition when he saw one.

My uncle struggled there for six or seven years, never with any prospect of coming off the bread line. It all came to a sudden end when, for reasons never explained, he tried to syphon petrol from one car to another by candlelight in the wooden barn. My parents never talked much about that. Walter gave up and became a Catholic priest.

I went back there much later when we were living in Kingston and doing a lot of riding; I saw an advertisement in Horse and Hound for a mock hunt run by the Garth and South Berks with the meet to be held at Whitcalls farm. I suppose it was nearly fifty years since I had been there and I couldn't wait.

The farmhouse had shrunk as is the way of things – it was little more than a cottage. The cherry orchard and the ducks had all vanished; in their place were some large bits of concrete equipment. What were still there were the flints; the field in which we parked was practically paved with them. One could almost feel the toil which Boxer had put into ploughing. It would have been easy to weep, especially as there was not much evidence that the farm was doing any better under the new regime. Anyway we had a thoroughly enjoyable afternoon's riding.

CHAPTER 4

St Augustines 1937–1942

Around my eighth birthday it was decided that I should go to boarding school. A lot of research went into it and my parents set out on a tour of inspection of Catholic prep schools. I don't know how many they visited but it ended up as a choice between Worth in Sussex and St Augustine's in Ramsgate, both run by Benedictine monks though from different foundations. By the autumn (I was eight and a half by then) it was settled that I should go to St Augustine's.

Up to that time I had been taught at home by my mother, who had got me well up to the standard the school required. What I was short of, was any of the social skills needed if I was going to be pitched into a class of twenty or thirty boys.

In the mid-1930s life in the country was fairly isolated. Round us for example there was only one bus route - into Reading - and there were no families we were friendly with closer than two or three miles. In those days, using the car as a taxi service for the children simply wasn't contemplated.

So it happened that the only friend I saw regularly was called Donald and his background was a sad one. His father had been trying to set up a business as a wholesale tea merchant but, before he had got very far with it, contracted an infection on a business trip to Reading. This turned into pneumonia and he died. Donald's own problem was that he was mentally impaired – not to the extent of needing medical treatment but serious enough that he was going to find it difficult to look after himself in later life. So my relationship with Donald was unusual.

At intervals during that summer, my grandmother, aunt and parents took to asking me if I was looking forward to going to school. I suppose a measured response would have been that I had absolutely no experience of what school was like, but if it was anything like the parties I had been to, I didn't think I would much care for it; that in any case it was two hundred miles away and I had never been away from home before. As it was, I expect I just grunted.

St Augustine's Abbey School was in the centre of Ramsgate; there were a number of schools in this area, known as the Isle of Thanet. Schooling in the area was sold to prospective parents on the basis that it was especially healthy; loads of sea air and a direct line to the North Pole with no intervening land, giving a bracing and activity inducing climate.

In September 1937, my mother and I set out for Ramsgate. It was a long journey, not shortened by my mother's depression. An hour up to London, crossing to Victoria from Paddington, and an interminable journey to Ramsgate. I didn't enjoy it but it was a new experience. The school, when we got there, was built in the grounds of Pugin's Abbey and Grange. It was run on the lines of a boot camp.

We slept in individual cubicles in a large dormitory. In the morning, we were called by the bell. Item one was a cold shower – we rushed through at high speed. Then it was dressing quickly and down for breakfast. This was usually inedible and was followed by teeth cleaning and gargling gargle was a solution of permanganate of potash, normally used as a mahogany dye for timber. It was lethal if it got near your clothes and was not much fun to gargle with.

My parents inadvertently introduced a feature of peculiar horror into my life. I imagine, because TB had loomed so large in their lives, they were terrified of weight loss (which went with it) so I was fat and they wanted me to stay that way. The school food was fairly disastrous but the remedy was worse – a raw egg perfunctorily beaten up in milk every morning at eleven was the official response to requests for dietary supplements. I can still remember gagging on it and I lost weight fairly rapidly.

Lessons took up a large part of the day and in some ways were the least testing part of it. My mother had been very thorough with her home education so I was actually ahead of most of the others and didn't have to struggle too hard.

The school uniform was shorts and a roll-neck sweater, comfy and sensible enough, but on Sundays we went to choral high mass in the abbey and were dressed in suits and shirts with Eton collars. As a fashion, they had been around for fifty odd years and had come to the end of their run. They were fully starched and about three inches deep, worn over the jacket. They required a tie which, once the collar was in place was completely unadjustable. Basically it was a nightmare to put on and after a few washings, the edge of the collar became serrated and any movement caused them to saw into one's neck. They gave one a curiously smug and self-satisfied appearance as can be seen in photographs of the period, mainly because of the need to keep one's head rigidly still to avoid the sawing effect.

I suppose that by the age of nine, one's taste in architecture is not fully formed but I remember the abbey fondly; it was dark and mysterious, given an opulent look by the gilt on the candlesticks and the other ornaments. Totally different, as I was to discover, from the abbey at Downside, which remained austere but brightly lit on the dullest days.

We were required to act as acolytes at high mass, names being entered on a rota. Basically, this meant standing around holding candlesticks with lighted candles, occasionally moving from one part of the sanctuary to another, endeavouring to do as little damage as possible with the candles, which were large and unstable.

On one occasion I managed to introduce a bit of variety. I had completely forgotten I was on the rota and suddenly realised that I had about a minute to be on parade. I needed a cassock, a black smock reaching right down to the ankles. I rushed into the vestry where they were stored, grabbed the first one that came to hand and sprinted down to the abbey. I just made it but there was a hitch; the cassock was made for someone two foot taller than me. The only solution was to hold the candlestick in one hand, quite testing in itself, and hold up the surplus material in the other.

I suppose I looked like a pantomime dame. It had a bad effect on the choir. One of the younger monks started to giggle and it spread. I remember catching the eye of Father Anselm, one of the senior (and severer monks); he looked at me reproachfully, clearly struggling with his emotions.

As well as high mass, Sunday was walk day. About thirty of us juniors would set out in the charge of some of the senior boys (thirteen year olds). We walked in crocodile (two by two) along the pavement. Once we were clear of the school, things relaxed a bit although we still kept to crocodile formation.

One Sunday we went for a walk along the cliffs. There was a fence about a yard from the edge, presumably to stop livestock going over. We walked outside it, between the fence and the cliff edge, with a drop of about two hundred feet to our left. Then we came to a gap where the cliff had crumbled and there was a two foot gap to jump over. The seniors held out a hand to guide us and we all got over, but it was a miracle no one panicked. I wonder what the school would have said at an inquest.

I was obsessed with aeroplanes at that time. My father had taken us to see a friend of his from way back who was the widow of the commander of the R101. This was the British airship built to show the Germans (with their Zeppelins) that Britain ruled the skies. Unfortunately it crashed in France on its maiden flight with huge loss of life and it proved the end of British interest in airships. This friend was living with her two sons who had built the most amazing model aircraft, about five feet long, bigger than anything I had ever contemplated and I was totally fired with enthusiasm. My own models were nothing like the size of theirs and I couldn't wait to try and emulate them. Four or five years later they both joined Bomber Command and I heard they were killed over Germany.

There were some interesting aeroplanes around; I used to see the JU52's (a German rival to the Dakota, unusual in having three engines) flying low over the town on the way back to Germany from Croydon, carrying, as I later realised, the diplomatic mail from Ribbentrop to the Fuhrer. I once saw a huge Vickers bi-plane dating from the First World War. Its maximum speed was about eighty miles an hour and it was used for parachute training. I believe it was also used at Dunkerque for a gallant and suicidal mission. Then there was an excursion at half-term when we suddenly came on one of the huge Imperial Airways bi-planes towering over the road. It had clearly had some trouble stopping and the hedge had come to the rescue.

Another half term, we went to one of the local airfields where someone was offering flights around the bay. I persuaded my mother to let me go, though no one else would come. The pilot was sufficiently impressed with an eight-year-old wanting to fly on his own that he extended the trip -it took more like twenty five minutes than the advertised ten. Both the pilot and I were taken aback by the atmosphere of barely suppressed hysteria when we got back to the airfield.

It must have been about this time that I was taken off to the opticians who diagnosed acute astigmatism – it meant spectacles for life. It must have been quite a relief for my parents who were confronting what they regarded as my suicidal tendencies regarding aeroplanes. It certainly meant that I wouldn't learn to fly unless I paid for it myself.

My mother and her sister used to visit at each half term. Half-terms were different in those days, being just Saturday and Sunday out of school, but still absolutely the high spot of each term. It meant so much to me, that I think I disregarded what an effort it must have been for them, particularly for my mother who would have done all the driving. I have no idea what route she would have taken – it was about a hundred miles as the crow flies – and of course there were no motorways. It might have been a hundred and fifty miles of actual motoring and they would have been lucky to average thirty miles an hour. On the plus side I couldn't have been more pleased to see her. There was a lot of effort put into entertaining me, which I don't think was strictly necessary. All I wanted was to get out of the place.

By Sunday evening, we had usually exhausted the entertainment value of the Isle of Thanet, excepting always the lurid delights of the amusement arcades of Margate which, in school uniform, were definitely off limits, and were ready to report back sharp at six o'clock. When we had made our rather tearful farewells, we all had to queue up for a spoonful of castor oil.

I don't think castor oil is used much nowadays. Notoriously, Mussolini used it on his political prisoners, apparently with some success. I don't think there was any ideological element in giving it to us; just out-of-date medical theory with a dash of old-fashioned sadism. It certainly taught us to expect that all pleasure must be paid for sooner or later.

The teaching was tough and old-fashioned. I enjoyed it on the whole as I had a good start and it was what I expected. Some of the teachers were easier going than others. The only lay teacher was Mr Kent, who was a kindly man, who had served in the First World War At some point he had had to have the top of his skull replaced with one made, reputedly, of silver. On very special occasions, we were allowed to tap it and imagine we could hear a metallic ring. He certainly had a scar all the way round his head.

Then there was Father Robert who used to tell us ghost stories in the evening which were absolutely brilliant. He also did conjuring tricks, notably pushing match sticks up his nose and bringing them out of his ears. Perhaps it wasn't all quite as tough as I remember it.

One moment of great improvement came with the first summer term. Because I was fat and not athletic, football for me invariably meant being goalkeeper on the winning side, experiencing the delights of Ramsgate's polar airstream. Summer changed all that. Our cricket ground was excellent and I was one of the few boys who really knew how to play. Those two seasons before the war made all the difference for me, and certainly changed my attitude towards the school.

Me wearing my St Augustine's cricket blazer, 1939

Showing promise at home

The war started at the end of my second year. Arrangements had been made for the school to move to a village called Hemingford Grey near St Ives in Huntingdonshire.I suppose the whole arrangement was made in rather a hurry but as a safe retreat it was somewhat lacking, as there were bomber airfields all round us. Later on, there was a tremendous explosion one night which was said to be a Stirling bomber with a cargo of mines blowing up in the air.

Most of us were evacuated to Douai School near Reading for a couple of terms so we missed the excitement of the first winter at Hemingford Grey, when the Ouse, which flowed through the village, flooded badly and the school was completely cut off, supplies coming in by rowing boat. By the time the rest of us got there, the floods had all gone.

Looking back it must have been a beautiful spot. The house was a medium sized Regency villa with a garden round it and two large paddocks which we could use and large outbuildings which became classrooms. It had all been there for a hundred and fifty years and was incredibly tranquil.

I feel guilty that I didn't enjoy it more than I did – I was supposed to be a country boy after all. There was no semblance of a cricket field so that was a complete no go. Then we suddenly had complete chaos in place of strict discipline; I don't know how it came about, whether there had been some collusion over what the boys were given as Christmas presents, but there was a sudden influx of air pistols. One model in particular – it was probably relatively cheap – fired by the entire inner barrel jerking forward which made it almost impossible to aim at all and this caused a fair amount of damage and some painful injuries; finally someone got shot in the back of the neck and 'something had to be done.'

The quality of the teaching took a dive. Mr Kent had disappeared, probably retired or prepared to tough it out in Ramsgate for the duration. Most of the discipline of the school was in the hands of two monks, both notably difficult characters, one of whom was subsequently laicised – abandoning his priesthood, which was the ultimate recourse for any priest.

There was also a sequence of completely hopeless teachers who were essentially trying to avoid going into the army; one actually had the Military Police on his trail. There was another who finished his employment by throwing a volume of the Encyclopaedia Britannica at one of the boys, quite a feat in itself, but missed him and put it through a window.

Despite my grumblings, they managed to get me into Downside with a scholarship so it can't have been too bad.

In spite of the lack of cricket, summer at Hemingford Grey was pretty blissful. We used to make dens in one of the paddocks – frameworks of sticks roofed with hay – in which we cooked snacks with the aid of 'meta ' tablets on tin cans; amazingly no one set fire to themselves.

Then there was the swimming; we used to swim in the Ouse twice a week before breakfast. It was lovely, warm, slow-flowing water, ideal for swimming. I swallowed some once and was sicker than I had ever been in my life before. About two years after I left, I read an item in the paper to the effect that the monk in charge of swimming had actually died of swallowing it. So I suppose I was lucky.

Fifty years later, Susan and I went back there. The village was pretty much as I remembered it but the school had gone. So had the house and the paddocks were now a 'Neo Georgian' housing estate. Very tasteful.

CHAPTER 5

My mother's family 1930–1980

My mother was one of eight surviving children, so, as well as my father's brother Jack, there were intermittently a number of them around. My uncle Grant was the oldest and David was the youngest in the family and therefore the general dogsbody. As a youngster, I got fed up with the way the family used absentmindedly to address me as David whenever they wanted me to fetch something from upstairs, which happened far too frequently in my view.

Early memories of them mainly centre on Christmas Day lunch. Gingie and Audrey were living close to us and Walter was just up the road, so it was logical that the rest of the family should come to us. I don't remember any wives, it must have been before Grant, Frank and David were married, but I do remember my mother in considerable perturbation over the seating plan, mainly to avoid finishing the meal with Audrey in tears; her brothers could be quite intolerant of her.

I greatly admired David. He had gone into the Essex Regiment as a professional soldier and also was in the running to play cricket for Essex as a fast bowler. In fact, the choice of county was unfortunate as Essex had two of England's best fast bowlers in their side. A lot of other counties would have been glad to have him. He used to turn up occasionally and play in the net with my father; more to the point he sometimes bought me a part for my model trains, something I greatly approved of.

His love life got into a bit of a tangle. There were two sisters living in our village and he had got involved with, possibly even engaged to, one of them. I remember her as pleasant and nice-looking rather than pretty, and greatly liked by my family. Her younger sister, who was, at least by the standard of the time, definitely tarty, decided to put an end to all this and have him for herself. She was successful and there was quite an uproar. My grandmother expressed herself freely and (even today it makes me squirm with embarrassment) I repeated it to David's new girlfriend,, telling her "My granny says you will grow up to be a very ugly old woman." My family were quite capable of carrying on a feud without any help from me, and I do guiltily wonder if David's departure to Africa immediately after the war did have anything to do with this episode. It did rather put an official seal on things and I don't think his wife Pippa was ready to forgive me; why should she have been?

As a professional soldier with some seniority, David served mainly on the staff during the war. As soon as he was demobbed, he took his family off to Rhodesia. That was more or less the last contact we had. He corresponded with his sister Audrey but that ceased with her death. His son came over to England later on, and that was not a success. When Aunt died, she left her possessions, 'to be divided equally among my nephews and nieces.' By this time David's son had disappeared over to America so being rather at the end of the queue as a beneficiary, his allocation was an outsize pink nightie – so far unclaimed.

Audrey was tall, large, and temperamentally very timid. By the time I was born, she was still living with her mother despite everyone's best efforts to evict her. There was a spell during the war when she was called up to work on aircraft repair in High Wycombe and thereafter she went to look after her brother Walter.

In her youth, she had had ambitions to be a ballet dancer. She was totally unsuited to it in virtually every way but this didn't prevent her nursing a grievance on the grounds that she had never been given the opportunity to try. Despite all this she was a very kindly person and particularly good to me as a youngster. She never married or looked like marrying.

Before the war, Walter had given up farming to become a Catholic priest and was given his first job as a curate in Walsall. He had then contracted TB and towards the end of the war, after being cured of it, became chaplain at the Oratory School. This had formerly been at Caversham Park near Reading, but had fallen on hard times; the building was sold to the BBC and the school relocated to a house in a village called Woodcote , about three miles from my parents.

We used to go to mass there in the chapel - so, more surprisingly, did J R

Tolkien who came all the way from Oxford, twenty miles or so distant. My uncle had acquired a new black Labrador, replacing the one which took me for rides at his farm, and this one used to sit at the back of the chapel and showed its approval by thumping its tail on the floor throughout the service. Unfortunately, the family ability to pick a quarrel came into play and Walter fell out with the headmaster and left.

Next stop for Walter was as chaplain to a convent of nuns who ran a school for disadvantaged children at Croome Court in Worcestershire. In common with the rest of the family, Walter had not much time for neo-classical architecture, so the fact that Croome Court was one of the great Neo-Palladian houses rather passed him by. He was more concerned by the superfluity of statues of lightly clad classical gods and goddesses that decorated the dining room and corridors. These were thought to be distracting but the nuns seemed to tolerate them quite well. In particular, there were a couple of huge (and hugely buxom) sphinxes either side of the main portico where Walter used to conduct services in summer. They were normally draped in purple cloth for these occasions, which didn't really disguise their shape but gave them a look of raffish splendour.

By this time, my grandmother (Gingie) had died and Audrey had settled on looking after Walter as housekeeper, an arrangement that lasted through various appointments right up to his death, with seeming contentment on both sides. Audrey lived on her own afterwards and did not survive her brother many years. I had kept in contact with both of them, and Susan and I used to visit at intervals, but by the time I had left Oxford I had shed my religious beliefs and I wasn't brave enough to discuss the matter with any of the Edwardes's, least of all Walter.

Dispassionate debate wasn't their strong point and I was cowardly enough that I couldn't face the ensuing family row. This did make relations difficult and I was always conscious of behaving dishonestly with Walter and Audrey, although I suspect they may have worked out for themselves how things stood.

Matters had reached something of a crisis in 1958 when Susan and I wanted to get married. It was naturally taken for granted that Walter would marry us and for reasons I can't now fathom, we chose to get married in The Church of our Holy Redeemer in Chelsea. As a non-Catholic, Susan was required to attend a series of instructions, purely for information, there was no attempt at proselytising, and it may have been that it was because of this we were recommended to go to Father de Zulueto. He was certainly very likeable if rather grand and quite a lot of the time was spent listening to him dealing with the problems of various Reverend Mothers and the like. There was strictly no instruction about 'sins reserved for the bishop' which much earlier had entertained my father. Although in his case, he was actually converting to Catholicism so the instruction would have been more detailed.

I was uneasy about whether Walter might have doubts about the propriety of marrying, according to the rites of the Catholic Church, someone whom he suspected of being an agnostic to an avowedly lapsed member of the Church of England. If he did, he kept them to himself. Father de Zulueto insisted on giving the address which was a relief to one and all. We remained happily married for fifty five years, though I doubt if that had much to do with our wedding vows.

Two of my uncles died young; John Philip – he was always known as that – came to live with us when I was about four or five. I believe he was already dying of TB though my parents didn't put it like that to me. We had a summerhouse in the garden, really just a large wooden box about seven foot high and with one side completely open. It rested on rollers so, in theory at least, it could be rotated to catch or avoid the sun. John Philip had a bed made up in it, not surprisingly with loads of bedding. This was the approved method of treating TB at the time and in any case there was a TB sanatorium just across the lane from us. I was encouraged to keep away from him, though the risk of infection can't have been very great. Not surprisingly my parents were pathologically nervous about the disease.

Although my mother was very fond of him, his life was a mystery which I never solved, nor did anyone in the family ever speak to me about him. I don't know what he did and, in any case he wasn't much over thirty when he died.

The other uncle to die young was Arthur. He was the next oldest after Grant and went off to the war, probably before he was seventeen, and joined the RFC, the predecessor to the RAF. He did a tour in France with some distinction, (survival was in itself something of a miracle) and was posted to England for night flying to combat the Zeppelins. These were the airships that were bombing the civilian population of Essex and as far as London, including his sister 'Sis' – my mother – who was nursing in Southend.

He had been recommended for a medal for flying round a Zeppelin, having used up all his ammunition, shining his lights on it so others could attack. He died, as quite a number did, when his plane simply fell to pieces in the air; this was in March 1918; not very long to go. One of his letters, telling his parents not to worry about him, arrived the same day as the official notification of his death.

Arthur, on left, with 'Sopwith Pup', 1918

There was one story about him as a kid. My grandfather was refreshing himself in the Yacht Club on a stormy morning. A friend of his pointed out to sea and asked "Who's that damn fool taking a yacht out in this weather? By God, that's *my* yacht!" It was worse than that, it was Grant and Arthur sailing it. They had to be rescued by the lifeboat. I think this was fairly typical; they must have been wild as hawks.

The whole family had immigrated to New Zealand in 1908. I suspect money – or to be accurate the lack of it – may have come into it; also the idea that a young country might be better adapted to coping with the antics of Grant and Arthur. My mother and her father went out as trailblazers – I have the tickets and a picture of the house they bought. It obviously didn't work, maybe my grandparents missed the squirearchical society of Essex. All my mother told me was about riding her pony for hours at a time – paradise. By 1911, they were sailing back round Cape Horn by White Star Line and heard by wireless the news of a sister ship – The Titanic.

I kept a close check on my uncles, whom I identified by nick- names – 'my farming uncle,' 'my clerical uncle,' 'my African uncle' – Grant was 'my no-fixed address uncle.' This was certainly libellous in its implications, but he did move around a lot. He was famous in the family for his improbable stories; there was nothing improbable about his service in the First World War; he had won the Military Cross in 1916 for a single-handed attack on a German trench. I never heard him speak of it, which I believe was not unusual.

A number of years after the war, in fact after my parents were married, Grant got engaged to a Belgian girl. My father told me that Grant had confided in him that she was 'sweet and unspoilt.' My father said to me that, even at the time, he thought this might be an unrealistic view of someone who had been brought up under the German occupation of Belgium during the First World War, notorious for the atrocities committed.

She was called Chloe, though for a time Grant called her Clorinda. Of my two other aunts, Rita was a permanent invalid, and Audrey had transformed quietness into an art form. Chloe made up for them. With the aid of a family photograph, I can just about remember a family visit to Rickmansworth where Grant and Chloe were living. I must have been about five or six. My recollection is that Chloe did not get on well with me and made some fairly acerbic comments. These did not go down well with my parents and the visit was not repeated. Looking back, I think she showed quite a lot of restraint.

Grant and Chloe didn't feature much in my life until we heard that they had separated. I believe at one point they had been running a pub and according to my father, had drunk most of the profits. He could be quite censorious and no one was speaking kindly of anyone else. According to Grant, Chloe had run off with the cook.

The next we heard was when Judith, their middle daughter, got married. The reception was to be at a pub on the Isle of Wight. Grant was not going to have 'that woman' near it. Needless to say, Chloe was having none of this and arranged to have her own reception upstairs. Everyone knew of the arrangement and circulated round both receptions without Grant being any the wiser.

Not long before he died, Grant had a job as caretaker of the Guards Club at Maidenhead. This was the club I mentioned earlier in connection with Father Cuthbert. By now it had ceased to trade and the buildings were in some decay. Grant's job was to try and prevent things getting any worse.

It so happened that I managed to blow up the engine of an AC saloon we owned – it wasn't the only time – as we were driving down the M4 and we were towed into a garage just down the road from Grant. We headed towards the Guards Club and found Chloe visiting. She and Grant had been living apart for some time and fortnightly visits were about as much of each other's company as they were able to tolerate; a bonus to these visits was that Chloe could park her car in the ballroom of the club which helped to keep the moths at bay. Finding her was good news for us as we could cadge a lift home.

This bit of the story is really about Chloe as, after Grant died, she provided endless entertainment. At some point, she acquired a cottage in Cowes. It consisted of one tiny room on each of four floors, but it was looking over the harbour. Indirectly, it lead to romance. Chloe had signed up for a 'positioning' cruise on one of the Cunard cruise liners, sailing at minimum cost from Britain to New York where the serious money would be made by the cruise line, taking Americans round the Caribbean.

On the journey she met Hoppy – so called by Chloe because he had only one functioning leg. Chloe was pretty wide-eyed about him, which was just as well, as he was definitely predatory. In her view he was mainly charmed by her talk of a car and a house in Cowes, seemingly unaware that, as she put it, the moths had got at the car and the house was the size of a hen-coop.

However, Chloe gave it her best shot and with increasing irritation, they lived together for some years. Fundamental to life in Cowes was letting out the house for Cowes week. This pretty much covered the running costs for the rest of the year. Chloe had always gone in for this with great enthusiasm, on one occasion finding that the only place left for her to sleep in was the downstairs loo.

The system proved the end of Hoppy. By this time Chloe had become thoroughly fed up with him and as part of the preparations for Cowes Week, she got him into a home. When the week was over, she refused to take him back. And that was that.

Chloe could best be described as indomitable. My father had a story which must have related to her early days. She was at the races, presumably with Grant, walking along a passageway on her own, when she met what was clearly a bookmaker 'welshing' i.e. running off with his takings. Not a bit dismayed, she forced him into a corner and held him captive with her hat-pin until help arrived. The last news of her was at the age of ninety, conducting a night-time affair with a married man of similar age over the garden fence.

There had been a close bond between Grant, Arthur and Sis; they were significantly older than their siblings and had all served in the war, the two men in the services and Sis as a nurse, and this tended to separate them from the others. After the war, with Arthur now dead, the dynamic of the family shifted.

My mother in a pre-war racing car – the details of this photo remain a mystery! 1925

Frank was the elder of the other two brothers. He bought a farm near Dover. While not as desperate as Walter's farm was later, it must have been pretty tough. No flints but a shallow soil on a subsoil of chalk. This was the middle of the Great Depression so it presumably would not have cost a lot to buy, but making a livelihood must have been hard work. He was a clever and imaginative farmer; he ordered one of the first combine harvesters to be brought into the country. Unfortunately, it was sunk by a German submarine but he got another. I remember him lecturing my father on ploughing in the wheat stalks to create humus, which at that time was quite a novel idea and must have been exactly right for his farm.

I also remember, much later, after he had sold the farm, Frank saying rather smugly, about the new owner, "He's a very clever young chap and he's learnt a lot at college, but they never told him that if he ploughs deeper than about six inches round here, he'll bring up all the wild oats in Kent."

There were obstacles to raising a family at East Langdon, notably a well just outside the back door of the old farmhouse, totally unguarded and probably one hundred and fifty feet deep – this was the cliffs of Dover after all. As it happened, none of the children fell in.

There had however been one appalling family tragedy. Frank and Rita's elder son aged ten or eleven was knocked off his bike and killed by a lorry. According to family history, there was a ring at the door and his mother was confronted by the driver, holding the body, with the words "I believe this is your son?" True or not, Rita was completely shattered and never walked or spoke properly again. The burden on her family was immense.

Frank had a hair trigger temper and complete lack of confidence in people like bankers and doctors so that sometimes he simply didn't get the help which he needed and which otherwise might have been forthcoming. Thus a rodent ulcer ended up, probably unnecessarily, in the loss of an ear. An artificial ear was made, but without make-up it looked awful. The fact that it came off fairly easily Frank turned into a tease for small children who were lured into unexpectedly pulling it off – greatly to Frank's amusement and their horror.

Frank owned a Jaguar saloon; it wasn't exactly his pride and joy, but he did find it very convenient; he told me he never had to change gear – it wasn't an automatic, he just used top gear the whole time. This included trips around the farm, by the tracks and over the fields. On one occasion, he had taken Rita for a trip like this and the car ground to a halt; eventually he managed to fetch the garage, with Rita by now in a considerable state of perturbation, stuck somewhere on her own in the middle of an extensive farm. The solution, when help from the garage arrived, was perfectly simple though it was not a problem that Jaguars were particularly prone to – the air filter, mysteriously located under the front wheel arch, was full of grass and corn seed.

Physical distance kept Frank apart from the rest of the family. During the war, he was living closer to the Germans than he was to us, as demonstrated when a German bomber, flying low on its way home, tried to machine gun him as he lay perched on the top of a haystack.

Susan and I stayed for a weekend at the family home in East Langdon but that was a long time later. I do remember receiving a rather unusual going home present in the form of two large sacks of well- rotted cow manure which we stored in the boot, and reflecting that a rear-end shunt on the motorway would have produced spectacular and unusual results. That visit was forty years after the time Frank was machine gunned and nearly forty years after the time I was due to go into the army.

CHAPTER 6

In the army 1947/8

Not long after leaving Downside I was told to report to the recruiting office in Reading. The interview was very civilised and there was some discussion as to where I should go. Did I want to go into the guards? No, I definitely did not. It was reckoned that I might stand a better chance of getting a commission if I went to Northern Ireland so I settled for that. We agreed on my having a month's holiday. Had I taken longer, it would have had significant consequences as I was called up under war regulations, the last draft to be called before National Service commenced. There were two consequences; I could be kept in the army indefinitely but, more to the point, it entitled me automatically to a full grant at university.

In due course, I was summoned to report at Poverty Lane transit camp in Liverpool. It didn't raise any false hopes. Next the ferry to Belfast; it took about seventeen hours and there was a fight in the bar when someone got badly gashed. Next morning, we were steaming up Belfast Lough and the boat had become a bit more stable. Belfast looked grim. We headed off to Palace Barracks, Holywood, about five miles out of town. There were about two platoons of us, say forty odd.

The camp consisted mainly of barrack sheds built of

corrugated iron sheets on a brick foundation. The principal use of the corrugated sheeting, apart from keeping us dry, was as a surface for the duty corporals to run their batons along when they called us each morning at six o'clock. One could hear the racket starting several hundred yards away. It gave due warning that the day wasn't going to be a lot of fun.

I can't remember how long we stayed there, maybe five or six months, with the weather worsening all the time towards Christmas. There was much drilling, all very meticulously done, with a lot of screaming and shouting from the instructors. We had one secret weapon in the form of a lad called Clutterbuck, pleasant and slightly bewildered, who swung his arms wrongly. That is to say, as his left leg came forward, he would swing his left arm forward - not his right - the equivalent of pacing in a horse. As we all kept some semblance of being in time by glancing at the next chap out of the corner of our eye, being anywhere near Clutterbuck was a definite problem.

He seemed absolutely immune to any form of correction and the first solution of putting him at the back of the platoon foundered when we turned and marched in the opposite direction, with him now at the front, when we achieved a sort syncopated march worthy of the music hall. The colonel's parade when the great man inspected the entire unit loomed as the main hurdle and I believe the problem was solved by sending a somewhat puzzled Clutterbuck off sick.

The people in charge of us were principally the corporals, two to each platoon. Ours were both regular soldiers, one not much older than ourselves. He was tolerable but a bit unpredictable. The other was older, named Etherington known as 'Jungle Joe'.

He belonged to the Gloucestershire regiment and had fought in the Airborne Division at Arnhem. One of his upper arms was desperately deformed, the result of being bayoneted by a German soldier when he was lying wounded. He was as mad as a hatter but we all liked and respected him, despite his habit of using an air pistol to shoot at people who were slow getting up in the morning. The sergeant was a seriously unpleasant man, imperfectly controlled by the subaltern who was notionally in charge.

As we marginally improved our drilling and fieldcraft we started going on trips to the firing ranges at Ballykinlar, a beautiful area south of Belfast not far from the mountains of Mourne. Firing .303 Lee-Enfield rifles went tolerably smoothly without any evidence of great skill. The next test was throwing grenades. It was as foul a day as only the coastal region of Northern Ireland could provide. The grenade was essentially a casing of metal enclosing a few ounces of explosive. This was fired by a plunger, propelled by a spring, striking down on to a detonator inside a tube in the centre of the grenade. The plunger was held in place by a metal handle linked to it by a flexible joint and the handle itself was held in place by a split pin lying across it. Pull out the split pin and it was essential to hold the handle tight inside the palm of one's hand. Once you threw it, the handle flew up and the plunger would be free to slide down the tube and strike into the explosive, followed by a loud bang and bits of metal casing flying in all directions. They were simple and extremely effective weapons.

To make them work, it was necessary to clean the grease used for storage, off the plunger. Not fancying an afternoon in the rain cleaning and throwing grenades, some of the more robust elements rather skimped the cleaning. When they threw the grenades, the plungers stuck in the tube because of the grease. The grenades, though now primed and dangerous, didn't actually go off, and it became the responsibility of the platoon subaltern (as pointed out to him by the sergeant) to explode the grenades.

The approved method for this is to explode the grenade by shooting at it with your pistol. However there is a fundamental problem with this. It is extremely difficult to hit anything with an army Colt .45. Shoot an enemy charging at you at close range and he will stop and stay stopped, but to shoot a small object like a grenade, the margin between being close enough to hit it and not so close that it hits you when it explodes, is very fine. After two grenades had failed to go off, our commander called it a day. A commendable decision and a win for the home team.

We had some more trips to the ranges with different weapons. One was firing a Bren gun in a gas mask. This provided a lot of fun. It was completely impossible to line up one's eye with the sights owing to the protruding filters on the front of the gasmask. After some experimentation, it was found that only by kneeling astride the Bren with one's bottom in the air pointing towards the enemy, and with one's head upside down, was it possible to line the sights up and fire – at the cost of looking ridiculous and very vulnerable. We were all certified as passing.

A trickier test was firing a PIAT. This stood for 'Projectile Infantry Anti Tank'. The story was that it only been used twice in actual combat and that on both occasions, VC's had been awarded. The basic problem was that its range was supposed to be about a hundred yards but to have any chance of success you had to be a lot closer. Being that close to a German tank while humping round a large piece of metal was getting close to earning a medal in itself. It weighed 20 kilos and had a fiendish kick when the propellant charge went off. We had a defunct tank to practise on, with which we achieved gratifying results. It all came to an end when one of the platoon failed to get a proper grip on the PIAT as he fired, so that when it kicked, he lost control and the projectile went into the ground about twenty yards away and exploded. Bits of metal flew all over the place, one of them hitting the Company Sergeant Major in the face, giving him a nasty wound. Once again, a halt was called.

We had some free time in the evening, partly taken up with cleaning equipment for the parade in the morning. Boots were a special feature. It was possible to get a spectacular finish by burning off the polish with methylated spirits and then doing the polishing. The danger in getting it wrong was weakening all the stitching so that under the rigours of foot drill, the top could part completely from the sole. On a weekly pay of ten and sixpence (52.5p), replacing boots was a serious matter. After kit cleaning it was off to the NAAFI where the food was not expensive and significantly better than the (free) food in the mess.

At weekends, one could go the five miles into Belfast. We were not allowed into Belfast alone, although the dangers were nothing like they were twenty years later. The bus station where we caught the bus back to Holywood was in a particularly dour and grim part of the city. Great wide straight streets with large industrial buildings and in every doorway there would be two or three lurking figures, doing nothing but exuding unmistakeable menace. I don't believe there was actually any trouble while I was there and I was never threatened, but it was an uncomfortable experience.

On the other hand, the city centre was full of light and bustle. We could savour the delights of the 'Rainbow Room', so-called because it was lit with the most lurid combinations of neon lighting, where the food was not bad. Then there was the cinema. It was huge but one always had to queue – that was pretty much normal in those days. I remember seeing 'Les enfants du Paradis' – there was a good range of films.

Look up 'potassium bromide' on the internet and you will probably come across a reference to its use in the services as a mass drug to calm the men's sex drive. We had a variant on this. We all firmly believed that it was put in the tea when a new intake had arrived, to reduce the risk of suicides. Certainly we all believed that we became afflicted with a marked urge to pee at these times. And there certainly were suicides – I remember two in the four or five months I was in Belfast, the preferred method being to lie on the railway running to Holywood. As it ran straight and slowly for several miles, it must have given ample time for reconsideration.

Others found more sensible ways of getting out. I was friendly with Jeremy Thorpe. There weren't many other public school boys in the two platoons so we used to hang out together. He decided very early on that the army was absolutely not for him. I was actually in the other platoon so I discovered all this much later, but he started by having a dizzy fit on the scramble net on the assault course. This was a piece of equipment maybe fifteen feet high, so a perfectly reasonable place to have a dizzy fit but difficult to rescue someone from. The army medical treatment was pretty basic so they gave him some pills and told him to get on with it. He had some more fits and more pills, then after a bit he took all the pills at once having prudently saved them.

This had fairly spectacular results inducing a degree of panic in the authorities. Correctly calculating he was likely to be more trouble than he was worth, they decided to eject him. One afternoon, we were standing easy during some foot drill when an extremely elegant figure strolled past. Our repellent sergeant, incorrectly believing him to be an officer, called us all to attention and saluted. Was there a muffled cheer? I think we were all too envious. Jeremy gave a languid acknowledgement and went on his way. He told me later that it was literally the only moment he spent in the army which he really enjoyed. That went for some of us too.

Belfast 1947. I am on the far left, Jeremy Thorpe middle right

'Relegation' was the ultimate sanction since it meant that you went back to the beginning of the course and started the whole horrible process again. You could incur relegation by really spectacular incompetence although, as this also reflected on the instructors, I doubt if it was ever used. Where it came in handily for the authorities was as a discouragement from malingering. I was confronted with this aspect of it since I had had a couple of days in the sick bay which was not a problem in itself, but shortly afterwards I got an abscess in my middle finger.

Going sick twice would have been regarded as sufficient evidence for proof of malingering. I was sufficiently panicked by the fear of being relegated that I had it lanced with a razor blade by a lad in a neighbouring platoon whose qualification was that he had been a medical student (and presumably failed his medical exams). Better lucky than clever they say and I healed up well and retained the use of my finger.

CHAPTER 7

Still in it; London and Africa 1948

Towards the end of my time in Belfast, I was sent across to the mainland to attend a selection trial for admission to OCTU, an Officer Cadets Training Unit. The test was supposed to evaluate one's leadership abilities and I was gratified to find I had passed. The next step was my final crossing to the mainland. As on all the previous journeys, I opted to go on the Princess Victoria from Larne to Stranraer which, with hindsight might not have been such a good idea; about eight years later it sank in a terrible storm with the loss of nearly everyone on board. It was one of the first roll-on/roll-off disasters.

This time, it was only normally rough and we arrived safely; I made my way to Eaton Hall in Shropshire to begin a two month course. This was a lot more civilised than Holywood Barracks and one of the pleasantly odd rules was that, as we were notionally on the way to becoming officers, the NCO's addressed us as 'Sir'. This didn't affect the general style of the address so that the Company Sergeant Major might call you "a horrible load of useless rubbish" then, after a subtle pause, 'Sir'. I can't remember much about it, which probably reflects a lack of attention on my part as I passed out thirty-first out of thirty-two. The chap who came last was truly terrible.

Next day, we got our offers of commissions. Mine was the Education Corps or nothing, so I took it. It was a curious thing about my time in the army that though the Education Corps were presumably looking for officers when I was selected, I never at any point felt anything but surplus to requirement and that it was taking up the valuable time of senior officers to keep me occupied and out of mischief.

First stop after Eaton Hall was Buchanan Castle. This was a nineteenth century fake Scottish castle on the shores of Loch Lomond. It was spectacularly uncomfortable. I looked it up on Wikipedia and it has now reached its natural level as a picturesque ruin. I imagine the Education Corps had been short changed in being allocated the castle as some sort of headquarters.

Full dress, gloves and cane, 1948

Mercifully, I was passing quickly through on the way to a two-month course at Eltham Palace. This was very much the real thing as palaces go and moreover had been made into a most beautiful home by the Courtaulds. And it was in the London suburbs, within, as the estate agents say, easy access of the centre of London.

We were free to go to the West End in the evenings but full service dress was compulsory – peaked hat, khaki jacket, Sam Browne belt – the lot.

All we lacked was a notice stuck to our chests saying "I'm only nineteen and here to be ripped off." I don't think we ever were. This was presumably due to good luck combined with an entirely genuine appearance of being skint.

One weekend in May I was seriously inconvenienced. The regular course work stopped on Friday but rather meanly the authorities would organise some form of cultural trip for Saturday mornings, only requiring one supervisor, but keeping us firmly occupied. Normally this did not matter too much but on this weekend I had a ticket for Lords to watch Australia play MCC. This was Bradman's last tour and my only opportunity ever to see him play.

We were taken to the Science Museum. Our minder, the adjutant plonked himself down on a chair by the only exit. I made a preliminary recce, just like I had been taught, and went downstairs to the lower floor. I discovered that by coming up the stairs on hands and knees and quickly dodging round the corner I would only be in view for a couple of paces so that with good luck and some lack of concentration on his part I might make it.

Triumph! No one seemed to think it at all odd to see an army officer in full service dress coming up the stairs on all fours and I was past unscathed. I grabbed a taxi and arrived at Lords just in time to hear the applause and see Bradman leaving the crease having made a brilliant century. I never had thought I would enjoy being in the army.

Once the course was over it was posting time. Did I pick East Africa or did I just get it? In any case it suited me fine. The first stop on the way was the Suez Canal Zone and to get there I was given a berth on the Empire Halladale. It was old, had been used by the Germans for 'Strength through Joy' cruises and quite comfortable but infested with cockroaches. I got my introduction to exterminating them by putting coffee in tins in which they suicided. It turned out to be useful in the next year or so.

Arriving at Port Said, we moored out in the harbour and set out by lighter for the shore. Surprisingly soon, we were joined by a scruffy character and I got my introduction to the mysterious East when he tried to sell us 'feelthy postcards'. The troops showed considerable intolerance by dumping him in the harbour and then throwing his stock on top of him. I suppose it was one small nail in the coffin of Britain's relations with Egypt, leading, not all that much later, to Nasser seizing the Suez Canal.

I was posted to El Geneifa, a huge transit camp on the Bitter Lakes on the Suez Canal. There was a general atmosphere of lawlessness in the area. Gangs of Egyptians led by escaped German prisoners of war roamed around and carried out armed raids on the camps, particularly the Ordnance Depot next door to our camp. The defence was mainly in the hands of a regiment raised in Basutoland. The story was that they, being hardened warriors, were taking the war to the enemy and killing members of the gangs wherever they could find them, improving the look of things by draping the bodies on the wires surrounding the camps. I didn't stay long enough to judge the truth of this. There was certainly a lot of shooting. One night, I was walking to the unit library when a machine gun started up, firing tracer a few feet over my head, worryingly close but not close enough to overcome my entirely rational fear of diving into the ditch.

A few days later I was booked to go to Port Said, or, more accurately, to Port Fouad, the French Quarter, where there was a transit camp for troops waiting for a boat. Rather meanly, they had booked me in as duty officer for my last night in the camp. It didn't go well. The duty sergeant had been given a pistol which he was supposed to hand over to me. He decided to demonstrate it first and it turned out to be both loaded and cocked and he narrowly missed killing the corporal. I certainly wasn't going to have him arrested so there wasn't a lot to do about it.

My principal duty was to patrol the perimeter fence, looking for any break-in. We were equipped with a three ton truck and it took about an hour and a half over rough ground. We were supposed to make three circuits but, in the cause of getting some sleep, I settled for one early and one late.

In the morning I reported to the Adjutant in suitably vague terms. "What about the firing in the night?" He asked. This was the first I had heard about it so I replied "Someone having a go at the Ordnance Depot I believe." Then it was time for a hasty dash round to the guard room; there were quite a few bullet holes and considerable irritation among the guards. Needless to say they regarded it as a personal affront to be dealt with accordingly. I was relieved when my transport arrived to take me to the station.

Port Fouad was pleasant enough. The camp was handy for the beach and there was a cinema showing French films at the end of which a picture of King Farouk would show up, followed by catcalls and shouts. The French really hated him although I'm not sure why.

There was a desk in the camp manned by a couple of sergeants to whom we were supposed to report each day and check for troopships going to the right destination. My posting was to Nairobi, but there never seemed to be a troopship going there. It really was extremely pleasant in Port Fouad; the beach was delightful and the camp accommodation perfectly satisfactory.

After about a month I got bored and I realised that it was conceivable, though unlikely, that I would one day be missed in Nairobi. So I made enquiries about Mombasa instead of Nairobi and was assigned at once to the good ship Ascanius. We took a train from Port Said to Suez and there she was, lying out in the harbour. You could say it was what she did best.

TSS ASCANIUS

Of the three troopships I sailed on she has left by far the most vivid memory. Built in 1910 for the George Holt Line, the story was that she had been built for the chilled meat trade and converted much later and, somewhat perfunctorily, for troop carrying. This may have been a libel. Look her up on the internet and the story is bit different, namely that she was built for passenger carrying. Those early passengers must have been extremely tolerant and certainly not paid a lot for their passage.

The army officers shared a cabin for twelve and it was not comfortable. Accommodation for the other ranks was indescribable. In fact, doing my stint as duty officer I was so overcome with the heat and smell below decks that I had to bolt hastily up on deck to throw up over the side. Even in the cabin, ventilation was the main problem. At one point a fight broke out between a major and a captain over which way the ventilator should point. I was rather shocked when blows were exchanged; in theory you could be court -martialled for striking a brother officer, but nobody seemed very concerned and a deal was patched up.

We sailed down the Red Sea in calm waters; the food was excellent and much appreciated. For no particular reason that I could comprehend, we called at Port Sudan and Massawa, finally Aden. Conrad would have loved these ports, soaked in tropical heat and not much happening. They had a sort of raddled charm.

Aden was the high point of the journey. Ascanius was a coal-burning ship, a rarity even at that time, so we coaled at Aden. This was a ritual performed by every P&O liner sailing to India in the heyday of the Raj, but I suspect in those days it was regarded simply as an opportunity for some retail therapy and the memsahibs were not required, as we were, to lock themselves in their cabins while a gang of extremely formidable convicts loaded coal from lighters, supervised by gaffers equipped with short steel truncheons they were quite prepared to use. I saw at least one convict disappear into the harbour, after being hit with one of these.

Once the coaling was over we were allowed to head into town for rest and recuperation. The shops, which had flourished in the days of the Raj, when liners called there, were now in a state of terminal decline, or at least had turned themselves into local suppliers, so we headed for the beach. This was hardly a success. Our only doctor managed to damage his neck severely diving in and the rest of us who plunged in, eager to get out of the heat, were stopped in our tracks by discovering that the water, brought up from the Antarctic by the monsoon, was fridge temperature.

The monsoon began to feature in our lives as we headed out into the Indian Ocean. Ascanius was not an ocean greyhound; seven or eight knots was the best she could manage, less now that we were heading some of the time into gale force winds. The captain, well aware of our fragility, certainly didn't want to be left adrift on a lee shore on the Horn of Africa.

Even then it was inhospitable and it had provided the Mogadishu Camel Corps with their only significant success of the Second World War, when they had captured a German submarine. This had not needed any great military valour or skill. The submarine had run aground and all that was required of the Camel Corps was simply to stay out of range of any weaponry the crew might still be capable of using and wait for the occupants to cook in the African sun. "Captured by Camel Corps" made an interesting variant on the usual reasons for the end of a U-boat's career.

Anyway we headed due south at about a hundred and seventy to a hundred and eighty sea miles a day. Once we achieved a hundred and ninety and next day broke down, leaving Ascanius wallowing in a heavy swell. We all became less appreciative of the cooking which up till then had been Ascanius' finest, perhaps its only good feature.

Eventually we reached a point East and slightly south of Mombasa, and turned hard right. We gave up pitching, started rolling and after three or four days reached Mombasa.

CHAPTER 8

Nairobi and Dar-es-Salaam 1948/9

We caught the train to Nairobi pretty much as soon as we arrived. This was the line which, when it was being built, had cost the lives of hundreds of Indian labourers to attacks by man-eating lion. It had also been the scene of an epic bicycle ride by thirty Victorian ladies who rode from Mombasa to Nairobi; quite apart from the lion, pretty much up-hill all the way.

The train was an amazing example of bye-gone times as indeed was the engine. We were six of us in a first class sleeper made with splendid wooden Edwardian fittings. There was no corridor and the only peril we faced was from the vendors who surrounded the train at every stop, roughly every ten miles. By the same token, it was easy enough to reach the restaurant car or visit friends, provided always that someone was left on guard. The best moment was undoubtedly waking up early on the grasslands of the Nairobi plateau. We had left behind the lush vegetation and sticky heat of the coast and here the air was cool and dry. Dotted about were secretary birds – I think a kind of stork; they sat completely still, looking exactly like secretaries.

I felt some quite unjustifiable optimism about my immediate future in the army. I reported to Nairobi HQ and it was explained to me that, under the 'pass the parcel' regime to which I was subject, I would be posted to each of the King's African Rifles (KAR) units for a couple of months with a view to transforming the educational system of the unit. I did rather wonder what this involved but it wasn't explained to me. Perhaps they thought the two months at Eltham Palace had taught me all I needed to know. I was to start in Dar-es-Salaam (Tanzania).

There was no direct railway line from Nairobi to Dar-es-Salaam. Roughly speaking, getting there involved two train journeys with a bit in the middle by army staff car. My journey also involved, for no reason that I can remember, stopping at Moshi for a couple of days, roughly half way between the two. This was a small unit manned by a major and a captain. What they were doing there I can't even guess and in fact the captain was away, so that I never met him. It might even have been an army tourist resort. The only visitor while I was there was a subaltern who came to climb Mt Kilimanjaro. He went up twice in the week, or so he said; incomprehensible but not impossible. The major was welcoming, showed me round and how to get a drink – you signed a bit of paper and left it in the bar- and then he disappeared.

The following morning, I mentioned that I needed to open a bank account to receive any pay I might get and the major volunteered to help me find the bank manager who was something of a buddy of his. Moshi was really only a grown-up village, its main attraction being that it was at the foot of Mt Kilimanjaro, but it took time to find the right bar. The bank manager had clearly been there some time but was entirely receptive to the idea of someone opening a new account. He gave me a brand new Standard Bank of South Africa cheque book. He said "I expect you could do with some money?" This was certainly true; so he gave me some money; for the first time I felt I was launched on a proper career in the army.

In due course I went on my way to Dar-es-Salaam. I remember a lunch at an African village of hard boiled eggs and minute, delicious bananas. I also remember reaching some sort of frontier post where we and the car were freely sprayed, presumably with DDT, as a precaution against spreading tsetse fly from the game area into the agricultural zone of Tanganyika.

Dar-es-Salaam —House of Rest according to Wikipedia - I remember with some embarrassment. I was sent there without anything specific in the way of orders; I think that once more it was out of sight out of mind. So I absorbed the zeitgeist of the place and did very little indeed. It was an ideal place for it. The climate was warm and steamy. We lived out of town not far from the harbour which was extremely beautiful; unlike the town, which was not. Our barracks, looking a hundred years old, were large and airy and the individual rooms were huge.

We could bathe in the harbour, keeping an eye out for sharks which followed the ships in and sea snakes which had a fearful reputation but were never seen in my time there. Land snakes definitely frequented the area and the local pet dogs - dachshunds, descendants of the ones brought by German colonists, used frequently to come to grief, mainly because of their short legs and tendency to bark at strange creatures.

Black mambas were notoriously the worst but green mambas were not far behind. We had one snake hunt when the unit doctor complained that a green mamba had parked itself in a tree outside his surgery. This had reduced the number of patients to zero and if it went on, the unit health would suffer. Very much after lunch, we all assembled to make a concerted onslaught. Fortunately we hit on exactly the right strategy, making as much noise as possible and the mamba departed for somewhere quieter long before we got there. We felt quite intrepid and affected disappointment.

The unit was one of the battalions of the King's African Rifles – the sixth if I remember right – and the officers, except for the doctor, were regular army who had served through the war and were now continuing their careers. It must have been quite a pleasant existence with no obvious purpose in view, although that presumably changed five or six years later when the Mau-Mau insurrection started.

The battalion had a sort of family atmosphere, very similar I imagine to that of county regiments of the British army. I remember an informal discussion in the mess about the appointment of a new Company Sergeant Major. Among the sergeants there was one obvious candidate whose ability far outstripped the rest. There was a problem however. He had history. Every few years he was prone to going on the most appalling blind, which might not have mattered so much if he hadn't also become violent. This couldn't be ignored and on at least two occasions he had been expelled from the army. A week or two later he would reappear at the recruiting office, the sergeant in charge would accept his new name without comment as a completely new recruit and he would recommence his game of snakes and ladders. I like to think he got the post. After all he was getting older and everyone agreed that he was an excellent soldier.

The army naturally dislikes officers like me who are not directly under control – it can lead to problems. I came across two examples. The first revolved around a posting to a small offshore island where they normally sent a subaltern with a sergeant and some askari (KAR privates). They lived in tents and it wasn't a popular posting. The story was that one particular subaltern, having completed a six month stint on the island, astonished everyone by reapplying and seemed likely to have been successful, had he not accidentally bumped into his commanding officer, coming out of his club in Pall Mall at a time when he was supposed to be on his island.

The second case I came across was when I was in Nairobi and was required to act as escort to two officers awaiting court-martial. They had been stationed in a unit somewhere in the northern desert of Kenya. Left entirely to themselves, they had found a way supplementing NAAFI supplies –gin mostly – by flogging the unit's rifles to the local brigands. This was a policy of extreme short-termism as even the army in East Africa was capable of counting rifles, and their own troops must have resented having Lee-Enfields used against them.

I wasn't under anyone's direct control and I didn't really fit in. Being at least ten years younger than any of the other officers, they didn't even know where to put me, preferably out of sight, on battalion parades. I suspect the colonel sent an informal complaint up the chain and suddenly there was a brigadier from GHQ in Suez Canal Zone doing an annual inspection and I departed abruptly for Nairobi. I wasn't sorry. But it also meant the end of similar trips to other battalions and in later years I did rather regret not going to Uganda where I might have attempted to educate Idi Amin, who at that time was serving as a private in the KAR. It would have given a touch of class to any memoir.

CHAPTER 9

Parenting, shot-guns and other matters. 1949

I reported to Nairobi headquarters and was greeted with little warmth by a Major MacDonald. He clearly regarded me as another obstacle to his early and peaceful retirement. My views on him were similar and reciprocal. We kept at a cautious arm's length. I was billeted at the Nairobi Transit Camp which served as a dormitory for officers from units in the Nairobi area. They were mainly waiting for early retirement and doing very little. Gin was seven shillings and sixpence a bottle, about 38 pence in today's money so seriously cheap even at that time, and army policy seemed to be that hospitalisation through alcoholic poisoning was cheaper than the alternative of paying them off. The younger officers were mainly, like me, expecting to be discharged in a few months. It was a depressing place quite lacking in the battalion esprit de corps of the unit at Dar-es-Salaam.

Next door to the camp were two clubs. On one side was the Nairobi Club which was quite grand and prepossessing – and expensive. On the other was the Civil Service Club which wasn't. I joined the Civil Service Club. Actually it suited me very well. I was welcomed into the cricket team which gave me as much occupation at the weekends as I needed and midweek there were net practice sessions and, worse come to the worst, there was always snooker. Funnily enough, cricket also gave me a wider experience of Nairobi life than I could possibly have had otherwise. There was some scarcity of opponents so we had fixtures in neighbouring small towns and villages. More to the point we played a number of Indian sides – there were no African teams at that time. The Indian sides came from all over the town including one or two which were next door to the shanty town round the airport. It was a revelatory experience shown up in sharp relief to our comfy suburban existence.

One day I got an invitation from a distant cousin – I had been totally unaware of his existence – for supper with his family and a trip to the cinema. Did I know he was a brigadier? Though vivid enough, the details are strangely blurred, perhaps a case of post-traumatic stress. I definitely didn't know that, far from being a case of queuing for the one and nines, this was the East African premiere of 'Scott of the Antarctic', not quite the Odeon Leicester Square but definitely posh.

I had had a suit made for me which seemed about right for family supper even in rather elevated surroundings. What I hadn't appreciated was that the tailor had cut loose with the styling – it was only the second suit I had ever owned – and the general effect was a cross between Private Walker in Dad's Army and a used car salesman. My first intimation that there might be a problem was when I came in at the front door and Mrs Brigadier took one look at me and disappeared (with the rest of the family) for rather a long time to try and adjust their dress to cope with this apparition.

Supper was a bit stressful as neither I nor their daughter were capable of speaking a word. Then it was only a matter of summoning the limo, complete with pennant, greeting the mayor and burghers and finally getting down to watching the film. Not perhaps one's first choice to watch a hundred miles or so from the equator but was I grateful for the peace and quiet.

Much later I cross-examined my father about this abortive attempt at nepotism, which was totally contrary to his socialist principals. He rather feebly defended it on the basis that his cousin the brigadier would have been mortified if he had not been told I was in Nairobi. Somehow I didn't think so.

This wasn't entirely the end of the history of the suit. After I got back to England I sent it to some dry cleaners. There was a long delay in getting it returned. Eventually the cleaners said the police had got it. It transpired that there had been a burglary at the shop and the thief had unwisely chosen to put on the jacket. The first constable who had seen him had promptly arrested him on suspicion. It was now held as evidence although I doubt if he was being prosecuted for lack of taste. I didn't ask for it back.

Memories of that evening make me realise now that I had no experience of supper parties and, more surprisingly, had never met a girl before. Plenty of elderly female relations and possibly a cousin or two, I had plenty of them, but that would have been before the war when I was ten or less. I do feel my parents did less than well by me in this respect. They had made huge sacrifices to send me to boys' boarding schools but I had very few friends at home and only occasional school friends to stay. Girls didn't feature at all. I was kept well away from the village school and we didn't socialise with our neighbours who lived about a quarter of a mile away. Even with war-time petrol restrictions it would have been surmountable but I suspect it was all part of the theory of concentrated parenting, which had also meant that I was an only child. Funnily enough our neighbours had a daughter who must have been about my age, who turned up at Oxford when I was there, but by that time there was a certain amount of history between us.

I had a definite sense of grievance that I was subject to too much parenting. There were my father and mother both at home the whole time and at the beginning of the war my grandmother 'Gingie' came to live with us.

My father, looking healthy and happy

As far as I could see they were all devoted to keeping me in order and out of the nameless and unspecified perils to which boys of fifteen were exposed. So it came as quite a cataclysmic shock when, out of the blue, my father announced he had bought me a shot gun. I still can't imagine why he thought it was a good idea. I think he always cherished the notion of my becoming a country gentleman although I hadn't made a very promising beginning. But this shot gun!!

For a start it was sawn off quite short. The story was that the farmer he had bought it off had fired at a pheasant which had got up while he was cleaning it, in fact still had a piece of wadding in the barrel. As the newspapers say, 'interesting if true'. The fact remains, not many shoots welcome someone with a sawn off gun. There was a further exciting feature; one had to remember to pull the rear trigger first as otherwise both barrels went off together. This took some getting used to.

I don't remember being anything but reluctant but I agreed to have a go at shooting some rabbits. We lived in semi-countryside. The area had originally been a huge orchard and now there were perhaps half a dozen houses a quarter of a mile apart; hardly a cosy village area or open country for that matter.

I approach this part of the story rather circumspectly. I didn't come out of it well but there were mitigating circumstances. Anyway I was mooching around in a field which we cultivated during the war, when a rabbit started up about thirty yards away. I missed the rabbit but, in the field beyond that, I suppose about eighty yards away, a horse made quite a commotion and started galloping round the field.

There is no doubt I should have found the owner,always bearing in mind it was 6.30 in the morning, and checked on the horse. However there wasn't much wrong with its gallop and I had no idea who the owner was. It had been well off the line of fire and with a normal shotgun would have been well away from any pellets. Anyway, I thought it was making a fuss about a stray pellet. So I slunk home. I know I shouldn't have and retribution didn't strike till much later.

Life in Nairobi Headquarters was peaceful enough with occasional excitements. There was a youngish captain, pleasant enough but not the sharpest knife in the box, whom I knew slightly. He was in charge of allocating officers' married quarters. As always these were like gold dust. One day he arrived in total disarray. There had been a disaster; he had allocated the same quarters to two families. Words had passed, the wives had had hysterics, the husbands had nearly come to blows. It was reported that one of them, a major, was on the rampage ready to take spot damages. Major MacDonald was out for the morning, so there was the space underneath his desk vacant.

Fairly soon an extremely angry officer appeared asking for Captain Dunkerly. He was clutching a sjambok – a whip made of rhinoceros hide which was the weapon of choice for anyone keen to beat the shit out of someone, preferably without killing them. "I expect he's gone to see the married quarters," said I brightly. This produced a strange change of colour in the major and a muffled groan from under the other desk. "Anyway I'm sure he's left the unit." This went down better and the major disappeared. Soon I was able to report all clear and Captain Dunkerly also vanished.

Captain Dunkerly was very grateful for my masterly handling of the situation – I think his standards were quite low – and asked me to Christmas dinner. This was a kind gesture; I was certainly not looking forward to spending Christmas at the Transit Camp.

When I arrived on Christmas Day, I quickly realised that it was going to be a tricky evening. The rest of the party were the Captain, his wife and his brother-in-law, who was a police inspector. Relations between husband and wife had clearly reached a point where they didn't care who was listening to what they said to each other. There was also a practical problem in that the African cook had got absolutely slaughtered, was fast asleep in the kitchen and had put the turkey in the oven with its guts still in it. We tried slicing bits off the outside but it didn't really work. There was also some discussion as to who was responsible for the cook. Meanwhile the brother-in-law contributed to the evening by being called out to a whole series of appalling traffic accidents, returning whey-faced from progressively more awful crashes. I looked back quite fondly to my squalid Christmas in Belfast the previous year.

That summer in Nairobi was notable for my forming a stable, albeit short, relationship with a girl. The scope of it was also limited since it consisted simply of a partnership at mixed doubles; it was quite intense however. The background to it was that I had completely run out of form and been dropped by the cricket team; so I took up tennis. No one had ever taught me how to play it but I had a good eye and aimed at hitting the ball as hard as possible; and I practised assiduously. I think we must have met at some casual mixed doubles game and got on well. There was a big tournament that we decided to enter.

It's difficult to believe how I carried on. I can't now remember her name, never met her outside the club, don't know if she was married and could only guess that she was about ten years older than me. She was an extremely steady tennis player which was just what I needed as a partner but, more to the point, she was near saintly in her tolerance of my erratic behaviour and mood swings on the court. It was an American tournament; every pair played every other pair and there was a big entry so it lasted several weeks and occupied most of my spare time. This format suited us very well because the mere fact of losing dismally to a couple of incompetents (one of my off days) didn't preclude an absolutely dazzling display against one of the top pairs, as you never actually got knocked out of the competition. I only hope I wasn't too arrogant. I do remember that we had beaten all the pairs who finished above us in the tournament.

It must have been sometime in July 1949 that I got my papers for returning to England. I went down to Mombasa to await the troopship. This was the Empire Windrush, famous for having brought a whole shipful of Jamaicans to England the previous year. We were nothing like so distinguished a bunch; they were mostly like me, returning from National Service. Awaiting the Windrush turned out to be a long drawn out process as she was already suffering from the spate of engine breakdowns which culminated in her sinking about five years later. Apart from mild anxiety about whether I would ever get home, I managed to spend a few weeks happily enough in Mombasa, though the hot sweaty climate was trying after Nairobi.

The Windrush eventually arrived and we set off for home. I was sharing a cabin with another subaltern with whom I got on well but most of the time was spent on deck. We got near to some excitement with the news that we were docking at Malta and could go ashore. My cabin-mate and I determined that a trip to 'The Gut' – the notorious street in Valetta harbour – was part of every young man's education so were well up for it.

It turned out not to be quite like that; for a start, in the best tradition of the Windrush, docking time got pushed further and further back. It was nearly one o'clock in the morning before we got ashore and got a taxi. It turned out everyone had gone to bed. We drove up a long, dark, menacing street and finally found a bar that was open. The hostess was a friendly, rather maternal lady who, correctly diagnosing that there was not much money around, settled for a pleasant chat.

Actually I think we were too late, not merely in terms of arriving at one o'clock in the morning but historically as well. 'The Gut's' glory years, if you could call them that, had ceased abruptly with the departure of the British garrison and the island was looking towards more orthodox tourism. Anyway we had been there, done that and now it was non-stop for home.

About a week after arriving back in England, I left the army. I think both sides were grateful.

CHAPTER 10

Getting used to Oxford 1949/50

My father had only two ambitions for me. The principal one, which he put a great deal of effort into fulfilling, was that I should play cricket for England, failing that for a first class county. As ambitions went, it was...ambitious. Funnily enough, one of my friends at the age of ten did go on to play for England and in fact captained it.

Even when I knew him it was quite obvious that while I had a certain amount of natural talent, his was of a completely different order and he went on to became one of best cricketers of the post-war era. His name was Peter May. We played in a cricket net in the garden under a complicated set of rules which we had invented. They were long matches and it was quite noticeable that although I was a much better bowler than Peter, he occasionally got me out while I never ever looked like returning the compliment.

The other paternal ambition, which was much more realistic, was for me to go to Oxford or Cambridge. I am not sure quite why, as in my father's eyes I don't think educational prowess really came into it. Perhaps he felt he had been deprived of the opportunity by illness – or possibly by his mother. In my last year at Downside I sat a scholarship exam for Downing College Cambridge which I failed to get, then forgot to enter for the Oxford scholarship exams, which came later. I think the school didn't serve me very well. So now I was due to come out of the army with no Oxbridge place.

However there was some good news; because I had technically done war service in the army I was entitled to a full maintenance grant.

Fortunately there was a friend of my father in the village, a retired professor who had been a keen cricketer and was also a close friend of the former Provost of Oriel who had recently retired. Letters with the college were exchanged and I eventually got one saying they would accept my Higher Certificate (A level) results. Then I got one saying I would have to sit an entrance exam. Finally I got one saying I would have to pass an interview. So I presented myself one afternoon at Oriel and was escorted up to the senior common room.

There was an extreme air of peace and tobacco smoke in the air. An elderly don was woken up to deal with me. We went off to an adjoining study. On the way he suddenly asked, "Are you interested in fly fishing?" I had to admit that I had never gone in for it. "Oh you really should; it's fascinating." So he told me all about fly-fishing and after about twenty minutes said, "Well I hope you will be very happy here and do let me know if you ever think of taking it up." I promised I would, but I never saw him again.

Normally, freshmen, first year students, got a room in college for their first year but because of shortage of space, this also meant sharing. The sharing arrangements were organised by the Dean and, based on so little information, it amounted to luck. Two of the freshmen, who both became friends of mine were clearly put in to share a room on no other basis than they were both Jewish. As one was highly intellectual with a family history scarred by the war, while the other was a scion of the City of London only interested in sport, the result was fairly disastrous.

Because I had got in by the back door, I was spared all this and sent off to find lodgings. Lodgings really did separate the haves and have-nots. If you had money to spend, there were highly attractive rooms in mediaeval houses close to the centre. Sometimes it was not just money. Three years later, I was cross-examined by a formidable lady who was only prepared to consider me as a tenant if I was a regular member of the Oxford hockey team. "Occasionals", the second club of which I had been a member for some time, simply didn't cut the mustard. This despite the fact that to get up the stairs to the room, one had to crawl under a beam about two feet above the step.

Not having much money, I headed up the Iffley Road and found lodgings in a Victorian terrace with a young couple. This had very little to recommend it; it was about a mile from college and there was a general aura of boiling cabbage and drying nappies. They were not congenial at all.

Having secured a lodging, I made my way back to Oriel. In the 'High', I met Duncan Chisholm, also not very gainfully occupied. He had been a friend of mine at school; we had been in the same classics sixth form – it only consisted of about seven or eight boys so we knew each other pretty well – and also in the school cricket first eleven. He turned up at irregular intervals in my life, filling a role somewhere between Gatsby and Sebastian Flyte. Some of my best decisions arose from extreme caution in having anything to do with his schemes.

I must have been a bit incautious this time; I hadn't seen him since school when he had tried to persuade me to do my army service in the Life Guards, and apart from reading a newspaper report that he had won a bet of a hundred pounds by swimming there and back across the Thames in 'tails' from the Guards Club at Maidenhead, I hadn't heard much of him. This time he said, "I'm just off flying - come for a flight". I don't think he mentioned that the previous flight had been when he took the test for his licence. So off we went to Kidlington, about five miles outside Oxford, hired a plane and, apart from having several shots at landing, had a lot of fun. I had broken my first university rule - flying without the Proctor's permission. A touch of style I thought.

We had a cup of tea in Duncan's room in BNC (Brasenose College); it was a large elegant room overlooking the Sheldonian Theatre. The legend was that it had been occupied by Francis Dashwood in the eighteenth century, reputedly used by the Hellfire Club and was haunted by the ghost of a girl who had died in one of their orgies. I thought I would have settled for that - certainly less all-pervading than the smell of boiled cabbage in the Iffley Road.

This was 1949 so plenty of undergraduates were there to finish courses interrupted by having to go and fight a war. The university hardly seemed to have noticed that they were no longer dealing with kids straight from school. For example, all pubs were out of bounds, college gates were shut at 10.30pm (or was it 10pm?) and all guests had to be out by then (and of course into their own colleges which had similarly closed their gates). All the colleges were single sex.

Most of the rules were lightly enforced. There were only one or two pubs which the proctors used to raid and they were deeply unattractive. Our preferred pub was "The Eagle and Child" always known as "The Bird and Baby" with a picture of Ganymede on the sign. We called in there most evenings, with no unwelcome attention from the proctors. Similarly, climbing in and out of college became institutionalised; there were regular routes which were used more or less safely.

Occasionally help came from unexpected directions. A girl I knew, returning late from a dance, had taken her skirt off and was climbing into one of the St Anne's halls of residence when she got an unexpected leg up, looked down and found a young policeman doing the lifting.

It is difficult to remember quite how miserable life in Britain was after the war and for how long a time the misery lasted. Food rationing was still in force in 1952/3 my last year. In my case, this had the peculiar result that my landlady (I was once more in lodgings in my last year) was quite determined that I needed feeding up, so insisted on cooking a chop every morning for my breakfast, complete with a load of chips swimming in fat.

The food in college was dire and college rules stated that we should dine in college; was it once a week? One of my rare excursions into public spirited action was to try and get the 'manciple', the college servant in charge of catering, sacked. I had discovered that he habitually bought all the college supplies retail from the most expensive grocer in town. It didn't take a lot of imagination to work out what was in it for him. I should have realised this was a forlorn venture, the crucial element being that he always provided excellent food for the dons.

A feature of dining in hall was 'sconcing'. This was, I believe, a purely Oxford tradition and I ought to stress that by common consent, it only happened on, maybe one or two, of the tables in the college hall, among consenting adults and perhaps not every night. The idea was that should someone commit an offence against good manners - belching say - or any of an innumerable list of offences, like speaking of work or women or in fact almost anything, some public spirited individual would challenge him.

Then a note would be penned, in Latin, outlining the offence; it would go, for example "multa precor domine Mauritium Hussey quod eructavit".* One of the 'scouts,' the college servants, would take it up to the senior don present on the top table. If it was accepted, the response came back "fiat". I cannot remember what was said if it was refused, possibly because that seldom happened, although the Dons were rather hot on Latin syntax. * "Master I pray you punish Maurice Hussey because he belched" followed by as much circumstantial detail as could be managed in Latin.

This was when the sconcing proper began. The college owned some extremely beautiful quart tankards, eighteenth or even seventeenth century. One of these was filled with beer (there were legends of brandy having been used with fatal consequences) and the offender was required to drink it in one draught. A regular movement of the Adam 's apple was the crucial test. If he failed, then four more tankards were filled with beer and circulated round the table at his expense; if he succeeded, the challenger paid. Soft drinks were an option but I don't think ever used. Before anyone gets on their moral high horse, it should be remembered that soft drinks in those days were a lot nastier and beer a lot weaker and cheaper than it is today. A gallon of beer, more or less, hardly counted for much on the statement of 'battels' – the final bill for your term's outgoings. Besides you could always choose to sit on another table.

Ownership of a car was an important element in a university career. During the war, petrol was simply not there for anything regarded as inessential; now it was merely difficult to get. But owning a car meant that you were always the target for opportunists like me who saw an opening, usually by obtaining petrol for some venture. Despite the problems, we managed to go out of town to dinner in restaurants that were just beginning to flourish after the war. The Bell at Aston Clinton, the Swan at Minster Lovell and the Bay Tree at Burford were all just about in range. The Oriel cars ranged from a Standard 8, new but not at all grand, a vintage MG, a Morgan (new and very smart) to an elderly Humber inherited from somebody's grandmother. The back of this was furnished in buttoned grey velvet and riding in it left the impression of being in a boudoir on wheels, an impression reinforced by the very stately progress.

The pride of the fleet was undoubtedly a Vauxhall 30/98 dating from the twenties when Vauxhall were challenging the prowess of the 4.5litre Bentleys as Britain's top sports car. Like the Bentley, it was built somewhere between a farm cart and a lorry. Its description on the internet makes interesting reading. 'Top speed of 100 miles an hour; front brakes were optional'. We knew it as 'The Beast'.

Very occasionally we used to go over to Cambridge to play hockey against the Cambridge colleges. Whoever had planned the road system clearly thought it was unlikely that someone from Oxford would ever want to visit Cambridge and the journey was long and tiresome. 'The Beast' came into its own on these occasions. On one trip, we had to return in thick fog and it was bitterly cold. 'The Beast' was an open tourer, so, not so much cold, as arctic. One person was needed to sit up in the front passenger seat to check our position relative to the kerb which the driver couldn't really see. We took turns at that and the rest huddled down in the back and kept surprisingly warm. Did we really have eleven people on board? I can't think what else we did. I do remember there was not a lot of room.

A hi-tech feature of 'The Beast' was something called 'The Lanchester Harmonic Stabiliser' – you can look it up on Google – we never did discover what it was supposed to do. What it actually did was to detach itself at high speed and go through 'The Beast's' sump, thereby terminating its career as far as we were concerned. It was greatly mourned.

Across the 'High' at BNC, Duncan Chisholm, needless to say, had much classier vehicles; the first was an Aston Martin 'Le Mans' – like an MG but much smarter – followed by an Alfa Romeo reputedly raced by the factory in the Grands Prix in 1929, which had had a Hooper body of singular ugliness put on it. When this succumbed in France to an episode of priorité à la droite, he got an Austin Healey. I do remember the Aston rather vividly as the hood once came suddenly down on top of us driving at sixty along the Henley to Oxford road.

Just to balance the books and correct the impression that our expeditions were all fairly mindless, we did go to one of the first concerts at the Festival Hall and also a series of expeditions to Glyndebourne, although the picnics there did perhaps feature rather too prominently.

It was always assumed that I was going to read Classics at Oxford if for no other reason than that I had not studied much else. The first surprise I got was to discover that Classics, or 'Greats' as it was called, was a four year course. The first part lasted five terms instead of the usual two and one received an honours classification at the end of it. I have seen it said that this was the toughest of all exams - sixteen three hour papers. The course leading up to it was certainly tough, the idea being that one should become fluent in reading and writing both Greek and Latin so that, for example, one could study Platonic philosophy in the original language during the next part of the course. To achieve this, we were given a large array of Greek and Latin texts to read and understand. Mercifully we were spared some of the more impenetrable poets like Pindar.

One aspect of university life which should be stressed was that the actual terms were quite short - eight weeks each - and one was expected to work hard in the vacations. The modern system where undergraduates are expected to find jobs in the vacation was actively discouraged. By the same token a certain lack of concentration during term could also be remedied during the vac. Or that was the theory.

CHAPTER 11

All about Oxford 1951/3

The system at Oxford, as in many universities, was based on tutorials. In the second part of the course we were allocated two tutors, one for history and one for philosophy. This meant two essays a week and represented ninety per cent of our work load. Tutorials could be solo or with one or two other students. Going solo, one was obviously more exposed and the essay could not be skimped; in a group it was highly competitive and there was strictly no corporate spirit. In either case they were serious affairs and it was important to show some evidence of having worked at the subject.

Humour was not encouraged. One of my friends reading history, writing about a mediaeval lady called Alice Turner, wrote," She even sat on the King's Bench, an unusual position for the king's mistress." There was a faint twitch of his tutor's eyebrow; my chum remained impassive; there was definitely no giggling.

Lectures represented roughly the other ten per cent. Their value partly depended on one's skill at note taking. Some undergraduates were obviously very good at it and one saw them charging from lecture to lecture and beavering away at their notes. Even if you weren't very good at notes, some lectures were necessary. If one's tutor was lecturing, it was obviously tactful to go to his lectures. Similarly there were some courses of lectures which were essential.

In company with about seventy others I stayed right through the course of lectures given by Professor Ronald Syme. He had recently, by Oxford standards, written the definitive book on the period covering the end of the Roman Republic and the beginning of the Empire - ninety-five years - immensely complicated and with unusually detailed original sources. This was a crucial part of the Ancient History course. At the end of the last lecture he paused then said," Ladies and Gentlemen, I would like to thank you all for your perseverance; especially as I belonged to a generation that, on principle, never attended lectures."

Another course I attended was given by an eminent philosopher; perhaps it is significant that I have forgotten his name; the fact that he always wore a rather dishevelled jacket from a blue suit with brown corduroy trousers, contributed to an air of melancholy surrounding the proceedings. The real problem was that he had achieved some eminence as a leading proponent of 'logical positivism', a theory very much in the forefront of philosophical thinking, especially at Oxford, fifteen or twenty years before. This had now been superseded, discredited even, and he was compelled to lecture, probably for economic reasons as much as anything, on newer theories, in effect a recantation of his previously proudly held views. At times it sounded rather like a Soviet political trial.

A lot of the lectures - not by any means the least valuable - were highly specialised and had small audiences. One day I bumped into Stella Joyce, a friend from St Anne's whom I had known for the duration. "Come on Maurice, you're reading philosophy, there's a young lecturer I'm interested in and I want to go to his lecture and you'd give me support. It's on Boule, Frege and the null class. Don't worry we'll just slip in at the back, no one will notice." Boule and Frege were mathematical philosophers, sufficiently recondite that I wasn't even aware that they could form part of the 'Greats' course. As for 'the null class,' philosophers manage to have a lot of fun with that. Evidently, a lot of other people were in the same boat as I was regarding Boule and Frege as there were only about six other people in the lecture. We didn't so much slink in as bring the proceedings to a sudden halt – we were slightly late as well. The lecturer went ashen, "Stella, what on earth are you doing here?" "Oh," she said, "Maurice brought me along." I think the lecture may have fallen below his usual standard.

One of my friends, reading history, made a hobby of seeking out rather specialised lectures. He went to a course given by a very old don, Canon Jenkins, who was chaplain at the 'House' – Christ Church College. There were only two others attending and one day they dropped out. At this point the Canon said to my friend, " Time to have a glass of sherry?" So they did and it was much more interesting than the lectures.

At the end of each term there was a formal ceremony held in the college hall. Was it called Collections? The Provost would sit with the tutors around him and each undergraduate would in turn be summoned to hear what the tutor had to say about them. There was often some justifiable apprehension – it could lead to expulsion – and in any case it wasn't much fun to be told you were a waste of space. When the tutor had finished – they were usually kind – the Provost would say a few words and offer a limp handshake. We christened it 'The Presentation of the Dead Fish' – a sort of gloss on Der Rosenkavalier.

Most people would think being a tutor at an Oxford college was a very enviable position. Perhaps for many dons it wasn't all it was cracked up to be. In the first place, being required to teach a string of undergraduates of varying dedication and ability was in many cases not what they regarded as their proper occupation. On the other hand, competition in the academic world was ferocious and beyond a certain point pure research must have hardly seemed worth pursuing. Some took refuge in eccentricity.

The senior tutor at Oriel was known to all as 'Happy Hargreaves'. A considerable corpus of stories had grown up around him. One day, my history tutor told me delightedly, "We've discovered Happy's social life. Alternate Mondays, he has tea in BNC with xxxxxx (another notoriously curmudgeonly don) and leaves a shilling beside the plate as he leaves. On the other Mondays xxxxxx comes to see him and the process is reversed." In a way, the story tells more about the preoccupations of Oxford dons than it does about their social eccentricities.

There were other opportunities for fun. One of the undergraduates wrote in the JCR complaints book, "I feel compelled to make a formal complaint about the senior tutor. At one o'clock in the morning he was shouting and banging on the floor in a completely hysterical manner. Fortunately I was awake at the time, practising my clarinet…"

The college chaplain could be politely described as flamboyant. One day, Nick Power, an extremely elegant South

African who lived down the staircase from the chaplain, pinned a note to his 'oak,' the outer security door of his room, "Who will rid me of this turbulent priest?"

The term after I had finished mods was my sixth term at Oriel; 'Schools', the final examination, was seven terms away and it seemed appropriate to relax slightly my somewhat half-hearted regime of study. The college colluded in this, since for one term they were without a tutor in Greek and Roman history; I was farmed out to a Mr Holroyd in BNC. He was a kindly man who kept a cigarette permanently fixed to his lower lip and had one sports jacket with lapels which were a sort of nicotine colour all the way down.

I tested his patience quite severely, turning up for a tutorial one day in cricket flannels and clutching a cricket bag on my way to the Parks, the university ground. Worse than this, I economised on the effort of writing essays by borrowing a friend's work (he had done the course a year before). This would have worked better if he had also had Mr Holroyd as tutor and if his writing had been better.

As a result there was a tendency for my essays to be tangential to the subject set and, worse still, for them to incorporate completely incorrect terms due to my misreading of my chum's essays. Mr Holroyd did display a touch of malice in referring to 'manuscript errors' and on one triumphant occasion, a 'second degree manuscript error' which meant that not merely had I copied the term down incorrectly but my friend had spelt it wrong in the first place. By and large, we knew where we stood with each other and got on very well.

My philosophy tutor was a kind man, not terribly

approachable. One day (I think we had been struggling for several weeks with the first three pages of Kant's 'Introduction to the Critique of Pure Reason,'), I found the courage to ask whether it might be possible to slant some of the work more in the direction of the questions we might be set in the exam. He was quite fierce. "My job is to teach you philosophy, not to teach you how to pass exams." Did I hear a murmur of 'God help me'?

On the whole I enjoyed studying philosophy far more than flogging my way through Greek and Latin texts as I had done in 'mods.' One advantage was that we did not have the sheer bulk of reading to do, compared with, say, English Literature. The other was that the quality of the writing was very high. Bertrand Russell, Gilbert Ryle, A. J. Ayer, Locke and Hume were all a pleasure to read.

Aside from work there were a lot of things to do at Oxford. I had a close up glimpse of politics. I had been walking down the platform at Paddington looking for a seat on the train to Oxford, when a voice said, "Hello, Maurice" and it was Jeremy Thorpe, pulling the politician's trick of instant face recognition. So we re-established casual contact – not on the train, he was travelling first class, but once we got back to Oxford.

Jeremy of course was in the thick of Oxford politics, especially involved with the Liberal Party and a situation arose which landed on my doorstep.

Norman St John Stevas had been President of the Cambridge Union, and now, coming to study in Oxford, apparently fancied becoming President of the Oxford Union as well. Jeremy and another friend of his who happened to be in Oriel cobbled together a largely factitious crusade, "Stop St John Stevas." For reasons which seemed good at the time, it was regarded as crucial to stop him first becoming President of the University Liberal Club at a forthcoming election.

Jeremy's Oriel friend (he was someone I personally disliked) was put in charge of organising a large supply of new members for the Liberal Club (by any means short of offering actual cash), all prepared to vote against Stevas and for no other purpose. It became almost impossible to leave one's room without being solicited to join the Liberals. I felt superior enough not to wish to have any part in it.

At the end of all this Stevas failed to become President of the Liberals and had to make do with becoming secretary of the Oxford Union rather than President.

There were a couple of large cinemas in Oxford which were pretty much like cinemas anywhere else at the time. There was also the Scala. It was situated up from Worcester College, say the top end of Walton Street. I'm not sure the concept of an Arts Theatre had been invented then; in any case it hardly did justice to the Scala's particular brand of seediness. I remember it as being small for the time but still a lot bigger than one gets in a multiplex today. There had been a huge outpouring of really excellent films since the war - British, Italian, and French aimed at something more than minority markets, and here there was a large captive audience. We used to rush off to see the latest Jean Gabin or Fellini or whatever - there seemed to be a limitless supply of films about brain damaged French peasants totally preoccupied with murder and incest. I remember 'La Ferme du Pendu,' pretty much exactly what it says on the tin.

The audience was entirely undergraduate and pretty tolerant; I remember going to a dark film with a lot of rain – was it 'Odd Man Out'? – and every time it rained in the film the friend I was with (he was in a somewhat elevated mood) would put up his umbrella. We survived, just about.

The feature which at the time set the Scala apart from every other cinema I had been to was the provision of double seats. There weren't a lot – two dozen at the most – but they could not be taken lightly. They were clearly meant for two; on the other hand they were narrow, by modern standards exceptionally so; if you shared one it was highly desirable that you knew each other pretty well. I'm not sure what their function was intended to be, but I don't think they achieved it. When the cinema was full they seemed to be the only ones available. This happened quite often. So it did make one's choice of companion something to be made with caution. Girls tended to view them with suspicion; choosing one could be viewed as a declaration of intent. The worst situation was if one's companion headed for the last single seat and you were left to sit – alone and vulnerable – in the double.

Punting on the Cherwell was a great way of spending a summer afternoon. The college had its own punts, which were readily available, particularly if you were using them at a time when most people were attending lectures. You could go upstream or downstream. There were problems with the latter; in the first place there was a weir which could not easily be by-passed, so one could not go far and, secondly, there was Parson's Pleasure.

This was situated on a slight bulge in the river and provided for nude male bathing. I never heard of it being anything but well-behaved but it was certainly disconcerting to come on suddenly. I believe that, after my time and presumably with a nod towards the equal opportunity laws, they established Dame's Delight for women, a suitable distance away. In the nineteen – nineties both ceased to function.

So upstream it was and there was virtually no limit to how far one went. It was quite good exercise and there was scope for a degree of elegance in technique, particularly in not dropping wet weed on the passengers or in falling in oneself. It was a source of some regret that the skill acquired didn't count towards a degree. Time for a picnic and then home.

There were parties but probably fewer than might have been expected. Finance came into it and in any case there didn't seem a lot of point in seeking new acquaintances when one already had plenty of close friends. Perhaps there were more parties in the women's colleges since they were disadvantaged by the system of segregation and the fact that women students were still in quite a small minority.

It must have been at one of these that my past as a budding sportsman came back to haunt me. I suppose I must carelessly have made some remark identifying where I had been brought up, when the girl I was being introduced to suddenly upped the volume, "You shot my horse!" She couldn't have been fiercer if she had been accusing me of being the absent father of her child, although I suppose that might not have come as such a complete surprise, or at any rate I would have been less likely to have forgotten all about it, than the episode of the sawn-off shotgun and the horse in the field at Crossways.

'And how is he now?' was the best I could manage but as it had happened five or six years previously, that was not necessarily likely to be relevant. I don't imagine our renewal ended happily but probably short of physical violence.

At some time during my first year I was approached by the President of the Junior Common Room, Laurence Verney. This rather grand title merely meant that he had been elected to represent the undergraduates in any matter involving them as a body. Basically this meant organising the college dance.

I was slightly intimidated; after all very few people indeed have a railway station named after them – in this case, Verney Junction on the Metropolitan line. We used to go and play a cricket match there each year. I cannot for the life of me think why either he or I thought it was a good idea to get *me* to run the dance; perhaps I was the only option left.

I was handed the fund and accounts by the previous secretary. He had come back to Oriel after serving in the Fleet Air Arm during the war, flying Swordfish torpedo bombers – eighty mile an hour 'Stringbags' – against the might of the German navy. There was a strong presumption of insanity against anyone from that branch of the service and he certainly had a broad brush approach to accounting. We had £120 in the bank and virtually all the previous year's expenditure was listed as petty cash.

This was to be a dance finishing at 1.00am rather than a ball, so the finances were tight rather than impossible. By far the most expensive item was the hire of the tent, dance floor and coverings for the passage ways.

One firm had a virtual monopoly of hiring out equipment for the college dances but I managed to find a another that was competing with them and saved £20, which was significant in relation to our finances. We looked set fair; unlike the weather.

By 5 o'clock on the day, nothing had happened except that the rain had started and I had gone up to the library to consult a guide to performing Hara Kiri. A quarter of an hour later the tent and trimmings turned up and we were up and running within half an hour.

Then the band arrived - could it have been Joe Loss? My only executive decision was regarding drinks for the band; the leader was firm, "It's got to be gin; give them beer and they'll be off peeing the whole time." The college did the catering and I came half way to forgiving my old enemy the manciple. To my amazement it was regarded as a success.

I have a photograph of our party at the dance: Stella, who pops up from time to time in my story, a friend called Peter Reid and his girlfriend, going back to his childhood days, called Barbara.

Of all the people I knew, Peter had one of the quickest brains, but he had a very sad story. He came up to Oriel having won a scholarship in modern languages, but the college, for reasons never explained, made him read Law instead. Except for those who (inexplicably) enjoy it, this is notoriously one of the most boring degree courses on offer. It drove Peter half crazy. His resulting erratic behaviour upset Barbara. They separated and Peter had a breakdown. He spent a year in Paris and the college graciously allowed him to come back to read a pass degree in modern languages; which he failed.

I imagine dealing with mental illness is always frustrating. Peter was a peculiar example. On a casual meeting, he appeared absolutely normal, but he was quite incapable of fitting in to any form of organisation.

As far as I know, he only ever had one job and it was not particularly exciting. He had met the owner, probably in a pub, who offered him a job in his firm, which made shelving and the like for shops to display Christmas cards. In the fullness of time, Peter was due to take a holiday. This is where a touch of insanity creeps in; he borrowed his boss's car (apparently this was quite usual) and then decided to stay away a lot longer than expected. So that was the end of his working career.

Shortly after coming down from Oriel, Peter married Maureen. They lived in London for a while, moved to the country and finished up in Thorpe-le-soken on the edge of the Essex marshes. Fortunately Maureen, although she smoked and drank as much as Peter, was one of those incredibly efficient people who keep the world functioning. She had a job, first as PA to the man running the Wallace Collection and then a similar job in the English Department of Essex University. When Maureen died, there was a big turnout from the University as evidence of the regard in which she was held.

Peter, on the other hand, never managed to hold down a job and was treated regularly for depression. They used to come to us for Christmas. We got an indication of what his condition was like when Maureen drove them both up from Essex in the dark. Peter arrived in a state of total collapse purely from the effect of the headlights of the oncoming cars.

At home he would start the day by doing the Times and Telegraph crosswords – it took him about fifteen minutes – then he would walk their dog, a beautiful Ridgeback called Simba, for progressively shorter walks. As she got fatter, he announced that when she died, he would have her embalmed and mounted on casters and he would push her mindlessly round the village singing Die Winterreise - he did have a pleasant tenor voice. Also, when he had access to a piano, he was capable of rather flashy playing, preferring to tackle the difficult bits to the exclusion of actually playing the piece through.

Peter Reid at the piano 1960s

We always enjoyed his company but it was also impossible to rid oneself of the sense of waste and the urge to tell him to get on with his life. We kept in touch – his letters were always a joy- but in 2013, Maureen had died and he was no longer able to cope on his own; he went into a home, the letters stopped and he died soon after.

Stella was the other member of the party. Quite early in our relationship, she and I had settled for being good friends. She was a great-niece of James Joyce and her other claim to being out of the ordinary was that, for some reason never properly explained, she had spent most of her school holidays at Castle Howard. More to the point, she was exceptionally bright and very good fun. She once or twice looked at me rather thoughtfully and said, "You know Maurice, by the time you're thirty, you'll be fine," rather as though I was a mediocre claret which was taking too long to 'open up.'

I never really got the bearings of this remark and, when I thought of it, it made me rather uneasy. What would happen after I was thirty? Much much later on – I had nearly reached the magic age of thirty by then – she said to me, unexpectedly, (although Susan and I had seen quite a lot of her in the previous few months) "You know you really ought to marry Susan" This came as a surprise; up to that point I had regarded marriage as something other people, older and richer (perhaps 'not as poor' is the better expression) went in for. It completely changed my point of view.

The last time I saw her was in Holland Park. Susan and I were pram-pushing and had paused for rest and recuperation. At the other end of the garden, Stella came into view with, I presume, two of her clients (she was working for Amnesty

International by then). They walked very slowly towards us and she wore an expression which I well recognised; it indicated that she had reached the ultimate reaches of boredom, may even have had her eyes closed in a trance-like state. When she came level with us, I said, "Hello Stella?" but there was not a flicker of a sign that she had heard and out of sheer laziness I let it go at that. I regret I didn't persevere. We never met again.

I played a lot of sport at Oxford - cricket, hockey,tennis, squash and occasionally badminton. There were inter-college knock-out competitions in all of them and I represented the college in the first three.

Tennis was a bit of a joke and our standard was not particularly high in any of them but we had a lot of fun. I captained the hockey team and I managed to organise some games outside Oxford. Most of these were against schools. I think the schools quite liked these matches, which were not too serious, and gave them practice. On the whole we got beaten but on one memorable occasion managed to beat the Charterhouse First Eleven and were most gratified to hear the games master giving the team absolute stick after the game.

Then there were occasional trips to Cambridge for both cricket and hockey. We were always struck by how different was the ethos of the two universities; no doubt they were too, but discussion of it would hardly have been polite.

Apart from college sport, there were games for the two university second clubs; these were known as Oxford Authentics for cricket and Oxford Occasionals for hockey. They were run like ordinary sports clubs and had fixture lists that were a cut above the regular college standard.

Membership was by invitation only and their matches were generally good fun. Do well in them and you could be considered for the University team.

Oriel was known as a 'rowing' college, although at that time not a particularly successful one. In my last year, we at last had a success in the 'bump' races. To explain: the races were an annual event and before the start, the college eights were all set a suitable distance behind each other, in an order based on the previous year's results; then, on a signal, all started rowing as fast as possible with the object of physically bumping the boat in front, before the boat behind bumped you. If you succeeded, for the next day's race you swapped places with the boat you had bumped. This went on for a week and if by the end you had done really well and moved up the river, a Bump Supper was declared.

A Bump Supper involved a lot of drinking and general roistering. On one occasion, Merton, round the corner from us, decided to set fire to their old boat, Viking fashion, which didn't go down well with the fire brigade who were naturally anxious in view of the narrowness of the streets and the proximity of all those mediaeval buildings. In fact, the senior fireman came into the quad, looked aghast and demanded to see the dean. The dean was ushered forward but unfortunately was not in much better condition than most of the undergraduates. The fireman looked even more aghast.

At Oriel, we were comparatively well behaved but I do remember setting out for home, (I was in lodgings at the time) on all fours at about three in the morning. A policeman loomed up, "Excuse me sir, are you all right?"

"Yes thank you officer, it's just I feel safer like this."

"Of course sir, get home safely."

It was a courteous exchange.

Two came back—Ben Bowring (left) and Duncan Chisholm.

2,000 feet and the other engine started to pack up.

"By this time we were in sight of the French coast. The pilot turned back and contacted Croydon by wireless. Then we started to lose height.

"When we hit the sea one engine had completely packed up. We hit the sea hard.

"We were 10 miles south of Littlehampton. I could not get out because I am a big man, but I managed to smash my way free with my elbow. I pulled the pilot with me.

"He was rather badly cut in the face and was bleeding profusely. towards us when this chap seemed to go mad. By this time the pilot had disappeared and I was practically out. I grabbed on to a body which was floating near my waist. I believe it was the dead woman.

"I tried to keep her head out of the water, but I had not got any more strength and had to support myself. Then we were picked up."

Thirty-four-year-old Mr. Bowring is an underwriter at Lloyd's and the son of the chairman of an insurance firm. His wife was at the Richmond Horse Show with her children when she read that a plane had come down in the

An extract from *The News of the World*, 1952

Duncan Chisholm appeared at irregular intervals in my life and one day in 1952 towards the end of my third year I bumped into him in the street. He tried to sell me the last ticket in a plane that had been chartered to take a party to the Le Mans 24 hour sports car race. I don't remember why I refused; probably money, it sounded expensive and I may even have taken work into account. Anyway I did refuse; a few weeks later, I saw a picture of Duncan on the front of the Sunday papers. The plane had come down in the channel and Duncan and Ben Bowring, the man who had taken my ticket, were the only survivors. They were in the sea for over three hours and I wouldn't have fancied my chances. They gave a harrowing description of people floating away to drown.

I believe the accident was disgraceful. The plane was an Airspeed Consul, a version of the Oxford trainer, and flying over the Channel it began to ice up. Rather than make an emergency landing in France, which would presumably have cost money, the pilot attempted to fly back to England with disastrous consequences. The plane belonged to Morton Air Services who claimed it was their first fatal crash. This appears to be incorrect as, according to reports, one off their Consuls had crashed off Guernsey in 1950 killing four people.

I went to a party at St Hughes with Duncan. The invitation was to tea with Antonia Packenham (later Antonia Fraser). It turned out not to be a great deal of fun. Present were a bunch of extremely bright girls who had clearly been honing up their conversational skills in preparation for giving Duncan and me a great deal of grief. We summoned up the spirit of Rorke's Drift and stood shoulder to shoulder against the advancing female hordes. After about an hour we managed to extricate ourselves, clutching at what Stendhal called 'L'esprit d'escalier' – the witty remarks remembered only after the pitiful retreat from the salon; and feeling considerably chastened.

I never met Duncan again. We narrowly missed seeing each other fifty years later in Cornwall and, by the time I got round to doing something about it, he had died.

CHAPTER 12

St John's Wood and Billingsgate 1953

My last year at Oxford was partly devoted to finding a job. There was a major difficulty – simply that I had no idea what I wanted to do. I registered with the University Appointments Board. This resulted in an irregular flow of letters, all pre-printed, offering jobs I didn't fancy at salaries which varied between the low and the derisory and all ending with the ultimate turn-off, annual increments of £50; so you would start with not-much and finish with very little indeed.

My father, with what must have been a heroic effort, organised an interview with Rupert Hart Davies who, at that time, was one of the leading lights of London publishing. He saw me himself (someone must really have pulled out all the stops) and we had a very friendly chat in which I talked myself out of any possible job. I think my parents may have been disappointed.

In the summer term I sometimes managed to get over to Henley to play cricket for what was grandly known as Henley Brewery. This was a peculiar team. It was run by the owner of the brewery, Bill Brakespeare (his telegrams were always transmuted by the Post Office into Bill Shakespeare, giving a certain improbability to his invitations to play cricket) and it consisted entirely of his friends, a source of considerable irritation to employees of the Brewery who were never considered for the team. I got in, partly as a potential suitor for his daughter (Bill always considered a situation in all its aspects) and partly because I was having a good patch in my cricketing career and managed to make several hundreds for them.

The opponents were almost entirely Old Boys' sides from various public schools – they mostly hadn't got their own grounds, while we liked playing at home so the system suited both parties – plus a couple of teams from the wine trade. The cricket was always very good fun despite the peculiar selection policy. The season usually finished with a match against a team from the Wine Trade, who were usually finishing off a tour in the Channel Islands and were described by their manager as considerably 'over trained.'

On the occasion I have in mind, I was in the changing room, unscrambling my annoyance at being gratuitously run out by my partner. I can't remember his name but he was Governor General of the Leeward Islands, when one of our side, 'Bunny' Lee, asked what I was going to do for a job. He was several years older than me, had been a prisoner of the Japanese during the war and now was an underwriter in Lloyd's, a proper underwriter taking on risks. I would like to think he appreciated my calm under trying circumstances but I don't suppose that came into it. It transpired that an acquaintance of his was looking for a clerk in an 'underwriting box' – one of the arrangements of wooden benches and tables at which underwriters sat and traded, based on the seating in the eighteenth century coffee houses from which Lloyd's originated.

In 1953 Lloyd's was completely different from what it is today. The majority of syndicates were small; this one had four staff in the box and one in an office doing the accounts and it was not unusual. So it will be appreciated that jobs in the underwriting room, as distinct from jobs in broking firms, were hard to come by. There were simply far fewer of them.

I was interviewed and offered the job. There looked to be some prospect of making money. Salaries in Lloyd's were poor but there was a visible route to promotion – the obstacle to it was sitting three feet away on the other side of the box. On top of this, there was an official policy of encouraging staff, both underwriters and brokers, to become 'underwriting members' i.e. taking a share in the profit and loss of the syndicate. To further this, a 'working name' had to prove he owned some assets – stocks and shares – but far fewer than an 'outside name' – one not in the business. In a reasonably good year the profits could easily be double one's salary. All it meant was transferring all my parents' capital to me to gamble with.

I think my parents may have been appalled but they didn't mention it and the family certainly needed some money.

There was one small problem; there were four seats in the underwriting box and the vacancy arose because the founder of the syndicate H W Edmunds was dying, but no one dared to fill his place until he was safely below ground. So I was despatched to a broking firm, Bland Welch, who were looking to take on some graduates. I was interviewed by Mr Cheeseman, the head of the firm. Under him, Bland Welch had acquired a reputation for extremely aggressive business methods. He was quite avuncular, "Always remember this is a young man's firm. Take my son, he's only twenty six and he's on the main board already." He didn't mention that the main reason for taking on Oxford graduates was to annoy Brian, his son, who had always wanted to go to university but had not been allowed to. The starting salary was £440 per annum.

This had all been taking place during my last summer term. I had rather deviated from a strict schedule of work, having discovered that no one in the City was in the least interested in what degree I got. However Oxford did bowl one last googly at me. About six weeks after the end of 'schools', the final examination, we were required to present ourselves for a 'viva,' an oral examination which was part of the final exam. For ninety per cent of undergraduates, this was purely a formality; they were firmly in the middle of whatever class of degree they had been awarded so the viva was merely a case of 'hullo and goodbye'. If you were on the borderline between two classes, the 'viva' could make a difference and was much more serious. I was on the borderline.

I do remember the two hours of waiting for it as quite especially awful. I had successfully banished all memory of such subjects as ontology from my mind and now I was going to be confronted with a panel of dons who might ask me about almost anything. I was called in and I remember a sensation of floating. I can't remember the question but I do remember the look of disappointment on my interrogator's face at my reply; perhaps he had claimed to find a spark of intelligence in one of my answers and now I had blown it.

I didn't bother to collect my degree, which would have cost eighty pounds for the ceremonial lunch which went with it.

Coincidentally, it was exactly the same amount as my 'caution money' which the college now reluctantly returned to me.

First step on a career in the City was to find somewhere to live. A friend of mine had found a flat in Grove End Road, just round the corner from Abbey Road Studios in St John's Wood. It had been Alma Tadema's studio and was full of sort-of-classical wood carvings which tended to fall off. The main room was the working studio so it was about eighteen feet high with a full length window facing north. There was a mezzanine changing room half way up which I was allocated as a bedroom. The fridge worked some of the time. It was cold and it all cost more than I could afford.

It was quite interesting however. While I was at Oriel there had been a vogue for some clever and amusing novels jointly written by Caryl Brahms and S J Simon – 'A Bullet in the Ballet' 'No Bed for Bacon' 'Don't Mr Disraeli' and others. Later Caryl Brahms had written some others on her own (with less success) including one about our flat. Sylvan, the friend I was sharing with, got in touch with her and she came to tea.

In preparation I had read the book; it was about Alma Tadema seducing the wife of Tissot, a fashionable portrait painter who lived opposite our (and Alma Tadema's) flat. It ended with her suicide. Not many laughs then. There weren't many laughs in our tea party. Caryl Brahms turned out to be dumpy and very boring. She claimed to sense an aura of unhappiness and sorrow about the place. We were inclined to blame the drains which had caused problems. Our exciting meeting with a real live author was a let-down.

Bland Welch had two offices; one in Sackville House, a modern office block in Fenchurch St. The directors and marine brokers worked there. I had been assigned to the home non-marine department. We were in the other one. This was a Victorian office building in St Mary-at-Hill, next door to Billingsgate fish market, down by the Pool of London. The fish market was picturesque but they weren't good neighbours.

For a start we reeked of fish. It was fatal to touch or rub against any of the windows because they were coated in a slime resembling rancid fish paste. In summer when it was hot, staff used to come round spraying us with what was supposed to be air freshener. The picturesque bit was the sight of the Billingsgate porters who wore cast metal hats with flat tops, on which they balanced boxes of fish. In the case of the eels, they were often still alive and trying to make a bolt for it, finishing up threshing around in the gutters.

I discovered quite soon that the Bland Welch porters standing by the entrance were there to check the time everyone arrived, so the scene was enlivened by the sight of city clerks in suits, sprinting through the garbage and skipping over the eels in order not to be late.

I must have got soft at Oxford. I don't think I was ever quite so miserable as I was for the first week or two in the City. It wasn't improved by the realisation that I had run myself into a corner, that it was nothing to do with anybody else that I was there, and that there was no satisfactory way of escape. In those days, people still remembered the days of the Great Depression; I was too young to have personal experience of it, but my parents remembered it all too well and had drummed into me the perils of being unemployed. Anyway I stuck it out.

The office party which took place about six months after I joined was a typical problem. People seemed to look forward to it; in particular one of the typists, who was about ten years older than me and notably predatory. She appeared to have me in her sights. The party was at the Great Eastern and there must have been at least a hundred of us there. Drinks were free for the first half hour so the start resembled what rugger players call 'a loose rolling maul'; thereafter they were at normal, eye-watering, Great Eastern prices. Having decided they didn't need me, I looked for an exit. These were all guarded but talking to the cloakroom attendants, I discovered a fire exit down in the basement and legged it through there. It wasn't easy and my dinner jacket suffered.

The following morning, nobody gave any signs of having enjoyed themselves very much. What I didn't expect was to receive a real bollocking from the office manager for not being there or leaving too soon. Perhaps they had posted the staff who checked our arrival time to do their normal job in reverse. They did know me quite well. Or maybe it was the predatory typist deprived of her prey who had shopped me.

I was put in charge of renewals. It represented the antithesis of the harlot; responsibility without power. We had a few business accounts; Bertram Mills Circus was one. The lion tamer had a personal accident policy for £100 in the event of his death. Even by the standards of the time it seemed a small sum to cover funeral expenses but it may have reflected the nature of his business. There were also a scattering of large private houses on which the insurance was taken out in the name of 'Duke of This and That' and 'Mrs So and So' for their respective rights and interests ; these provoked merriment but actually just reflected the preponderance of leasehold agreements in the London market.

After about a year in Bland Welch I got a summons to see the director, a pleasant youngish man who was in charge of the department. He began the conversation by asking me if I realised that I had only got into work on time twice in the previous month. I was genuinely surprised that anyone had kept a record of this but felt that saying so would only increase his obvious unease. I could sense that I was going to get the sack, which was no great surprise to me, so it seemed the right moment to mention that I had a job in an underwriting box waiting for me. This obviously came as a great relief and we parted on the best of terms which lasted all the rest of the time we were both in Lloyd's.

With H W Edmunds safely buried, it was now the time to introduce me into the underwriting box. The new underwriter was HWE's son Herbert David Edmunds, always known as David. The deputy was Mr Titterrell and there was another clerk Fred Folwell. Christian names didn't feature much but I did rather object to Titterrell always addressing me as though my name was spelt with two z's. Stones and glasshouses came to mind.

The default atmosphere of the box was one of mutual dislike. This stemmed from the top. Titterrell, the deputy, had joined the firm in 1917 and had been deputy to HWE for some years. He expected to be made underwriter when HWE died, a result which no one else expected and which, needless to say, didn't happen. At a lower level, Folwell was mistrustful of me as my arrival could only mean a downward step for him in the promotion ladder.

David Edmunds was left trying to impose his will on a recalcitrant deputy – not very successfully. He was basically a kindly man and had suffered at his father's hands. I shouldn't expect him to have been a reader of Philip Larkin but I cannot imagine a closer illustration of the line "They fuck you up your mum and dad." His father, known always as HWE, was legendary. There were endless stories about him.

At the entrances to Lloyd's, they kept huge ashtrays, two feet across and about waist high, with sand in the bottom; people used to nip out for a quick drag and return leaving half a cigarette or more in the ashtray. HWE saw no reason to waste these. One day a party of brokers tied a dozen of these butts together with cotton and watched admiringly as he casually scooped one up and trailed the others. He was one of the richest men in Lloyd's.

In those days, the lifts in Lloyd's were made of an open metal framework. HWE had been officially warned off from standing at the bottom gazing at the typist's legs as they went up. Along with spectacular meanness and some rather unpleasant habits, HWE had been a successful underwriter. In 1917 he had made £75,000 annual profit for each of the names, equivalent to several millions today. It was a complicated story and perfectly legal but the profit essentially stemmed from the huge losses of British shipping that year due to German submarines. One wonders why either he or the names continued underwriting after that.

Titterrell suffered from chronic depression and his circumstances did nothing to alleviate it. Apart from his (self-induced) problems at work, his home life was distressing. He had one daughter who suffered from epileptic seizures, thought to be the result of being dropped as a baby. He was severely emaciated, surviving on a diet of extra strong mints.

He was also a serious miser. Later on, the syndicate suffered big losses and I was concerned that Titterrell (who had long retired by then, although he was still 'an underwriting member') might become destitute and so despite the lure of settling some old scores, set in motion an attempt to mitigate them for him. It turned out that he had £250,000 on deposit at the bank.

Folwell, always Fred, was a much more extrovert character. He had served as a gunner on merchant ships during the war, including some of the toughest Atlantic convoys. He consumed more beer than most people and as he lived in Wanstead in East London, it was considered fortunate that there was no ferry sailing from Southend as he was frequently found asleep there at the end of the line. He and I got on pretty well over the years. I settled down to earn my keep, boring as it might be.

At the same time, my social life was not going well. My friendship with Bill Brakespeare's daughter had not survived a trip to Stratford when I took her to see Laurence Olivier in Titus Andronicus. It was incredibly hot in the theatre and in the interval the bar resembled a cross channel ferry on a bad day. I think the Brakespeares gave up on me after that.

I imagine many young men starting out in business rely on their workmates to help them make new acquaintances. I had virtually no workmates, certainly none that were suitable; as for girls, there were literally none in Lloyd's at that time. No underwriters, no brokers, even the companies which had offices in the Lloyd's market were not much different. There was a report that Ingosstrakh, the Russian State insurance company, which had an office in the City, had employed a lady deputy but it was also rumoured that she had been seconded from their hammer throwing team.

I had been working in the Underwriting Box in Lloyd's for about a year when I met Lucienne Xanthos. She was half Greek and half Belgian and, like my aunt Chloe forty years earlier, had spent the war in Belgium under German occupation. She was tall, slim, almost boyish, and blonde. She also dressed with considerable elegance.

I was asked to lunch by an acquaintance to make up a party of four, with the explicit intention of his getting off with a particular girl who had been invited. It didn't work out like that. Lucienne and I were introduced and started talking to each other; it went on throughout lunch; the others went for a walk and we went on talking. They came back and our host, who by then was getting somewhat irritable, eventually booted us out. So we went home.

I am amazed at how little I remember about the next few months or indeed how many months there were; I guess at least six and it could have been twelve.

That Easter we went bicycling round Ely – it had the advantage of being very flat – and stayed at the Railway Inn at Ely. It was not posh or even comfortable, a bit like a cash-strapped production of La Boheme Act 1 without the TB for once, but with the drunken chorus from the bar below.

Lucienne was keen on riding and had had her own pony, so on Easter Monday we went to the National Hunt meeting at Huntingdon. Amazingly, it was warm and sunny; we sat on the grass and had a wonderful day. In one race a horse had clearly bolted at the start and at the first bend went straight on, jumped a hedge, did a circuit of a neighbouring field, jumped the hedge again and came in with the others to loud applause. You don't see that too often at Cheltenham.

Lucienne was PA to Maurice Chevalier, still quite a big name, though well past his peak. He was starring in a new show and we were invited to the first night; 'drinks etc' before, and front stalls for the show. It was the 'etc' in the invitation that was troubling. We had to take enormous precautions to make sure I wasn't left alone with him even for a minute or two. As for the show, it exceeded all our expectations - it was truly dreadful.

My remaining memory is of a trip abroad. I had arranged to go on a European tour with an Oriel friend, David Corcos - Salzburg, Vienna, Venice, Siena and Florence, not leaving too much out. Lucienne had gone to Cannes, solo. For our last night in Florence, Corcos and I had dinner in a restaurant next to the Duomo. Afterwards, it seemed a good idea to try walking on the railings which surrounded it. We didn't get far; I suppose I was lucky not to break my leg and I did pick up some spectacular bruises; the train journey the following morning, from Pisa to Cannes, was memorably awful. I left David to carry on home.

I found Lucienne in a large (and surprisingly cheap) hotel and we spent an idyllic day on the beach, only interrupted by Frenchmen wanting to know what I had done to my leg. What they really wanted to know was how to chat up Lucienne.

I'm not sure now that I really understand the meaning of the expression "To give oneself completely to someone" but that was what it felt like at the time. One day I got a message; did Lucienne write it or was it mentioned in passing? She was off to join her parents in Rhodesia. I wasn't invited to come, and I think it would have been a considerable shock to them if she had turned up with an impecunious Englishman in tow. I spent a lot of time in futile agonising over whether to go out there anyway.

There were an awful lot of reasons not to go. As an only child, my parents were going to need my support, physical as well as financial in their old age. They certainly didn't need me to come borrowing the money for my fare in order to go out of their lives, possibly for ever. Deep down I suppose I realised that in the long term Lucienne and I would drive each other mad. Even then I didn't trust her taste for Peynet cartoons – you can see them on Wikipedia.

I had one letter from Rhodesia; she would have liked to remain friends and now I regret I refused. I simply couldn't bring myself to do it. I do wonder quite often what became of her.

CHAPTER 13

Helping Father and vice versa 1953/6

During my early days in London I used to go down to Henley most weekends, leaving London on Friday night and returning late on Sunday. This was mainly to catch up with all the jobs around my parents' house, but I also managed to find time to carry on with my woodworking hobby. This went back to Oxford days.

My last day at Oxford had started rather bleakly. There had clearly been a party the night before and I really didn't feel very well. As a corollary to this, I was acutely aware that my father was arriving in a couple of hours to collect me and my possessions. This would raise the question of the baffle in critical form.

In pursuit of anything which would keep me away from work I had become very interested in hi-fi. It was all new and exciting. Vinyl discs had only just been invented and up till then the limit of ambition for most of us was to pay a bit extra for a Murphy radio because, being made of wood, it had better 'tone'; whatever that was.

Now there were separate components -Acos cartridges for example -which one could play around with; I bought an amplifier from a man who was moonlighting making them. It was all I could wish for; it weighed about twenty pounds, had a 'line' voltage of 400 volts ("it could give you a nasty nip," he said understatedly) and was full of fragile and expensive glass valves.

All this was as nothing to the pleasure of loudspeaker making; well not actually the loudspeakers themselves, one bought them from Wharfedale, but the cabinets into which they went. This was long before clever men found how to make loudspeakers both small and excellent, so basically it was a case of 'the bigger the better'; which brings me to the 'baffle'.

The baffle is the absolutely basic way of mounting a loudspeaker; a large sheet of wood with the loudspeaker mounted not exactly in the middle of it. It works really well and is obviously very simple, but it has to be big. This one was five foot square and an inch thick (1.5m square by 25mm). It worked very well but wouldn't go into a Ford 'Popular'. It sat in the corner of my room in college and even there looked extremely imposing.

So with the aid of a rather blunt hand-saw and the college sofa as a saw bench, I set about reducing the baffle into pieces which would both go into the car and from which I could later make a cabinet. If nothing else, it cured my hangover.

I took the pieces home; at this date still where my parents lived, and so started a hobby which developed into making furniture, as well as ever more elaborate loudspeaker cabinets. My penultimate pair, made over forty years later, were made with a complex exponential horn curled up inside. At this time, what was more significant was that it did bring me quite a lot closer to my father.

As a family we tended not to discuss things with each other.

Certainly not emotional matters. Even my overdraft didn't feature. Woodwork however was safely neutral and at the same time something in which my father took a keen interest; he had a lot of unusual tools which he showed me how to manage and let me use his work-bench; this was made of solid teak, purchased at Harrods as a present from his mother, which I still possess.

Another hobby which my father got me interested in was photography. Like the hi-fi, it was not so much about the end product as the fun of achieving it. My father had been, and still was to some extent, a keen photographer. In those days, it implied doing your own processing. In my father's case there was no question of buying ready - made developer and so on. He preferred buying the chemicals from the chemist and mixing them according to published formulae. ID76 I seem to remember was the standard developer, but there was fun to be had modifying it, to achieve greater effective film speed or finer definition. These were refined pleasures.

We fixed up a darkroom in one of the outhouses; it was crazily dangerous. Like most farmers, my father couldn't bear to throw things away so there were plenty of light fittings past their sell-by date and electric flex with perished rubber insulation to provide excitement in a room with lots of water slopping around and, by definition, not much light.

Possibly in order to inculcate some financial prudence in me, we spent very little on equipment. The solutions had to be kept at a temperature of 68f (20c) so we made heaters of biscuit tins, sealed to prevent them emitting light, with low wattage electric lights inside to provide the heat - they did that only too well. There was one occasion when I saw steam rising from the sink where one of the leads (obviously the insulation had seen better days) was trailing in some water.

I tried out some ridiculously difficult processes; there was an early colour printing process which involved five or six separate steps, all at accurate temperature, each print taking an hour in total darkness. I produced one print but didn't much like the colour balance.

My father had several cameras which he was happy for me to use; a feeling I didn't entirely reciprocate. They were all plate cameras; that is to say the negative was a sheet of glass, one out of several standard sizes, coated with photographic emulsion and pre-loaded into a plate holder. This had a light-proof sliding shutter which you pulled out once the plate was in the camera and you were ready to take the photo. And of course you had to remember to put back the shutter afterwards.

Then, if you had actually managed to take a picture without fogging the plate, there was the treat of developing the plates, each one individually, in a bowl in the darkroom with a glimmer of red light. You could, of course, customise the processing and, in studios, the plates were regularly retouched by hand after development – in the process often achieving that corpselike look that is a feature of professional photographs in family albums. Not that there weren't plenty of amazing photographs taken on plates; it's just about why I didn't take any of them.

I had a number of cameras, none very expensive and some of them quite odd. One was called an 'Etui' – a purse- because it would theoretically fit in one's pocket, and so it would, using plates. With an adaptor to take film however, it was far too bulky. I used it for a long time and was very fond of it, but occasionally the exposure would be completely wrong. It took me a long time to discover that the shutter had been repaired and though it was calibrated from 1/250 up to one second, it exposed at 1/25 of a second whatever the setting.

Before we started buying photographic chemicals, there had been other visits to the chemist. At the beginning of the war, our chickens (there were about two thousands of them) started dying of a mysterious ailment. My father thought it was due to a mite of some kind so we went to the chemist for some nicotine (highly toxic). The idea was that my father would hold the chicken and I would paint its bottom with nicotine. We did it in the downstairs loo. It was very cramped and worryingly dangerous. Fortunately, a trial run proved unsuccessful so I was let off doing two thousands of them. It turned out to be vitamin deficiency due to someone interfering with their mash.

Few people today, living in the country, can have any idea how many wasps we had to put up with. People talk of the golden summers of childhood; all I remember is the wasps. The kitchen was a nightmare and having tea in the garden was virtually impossible. The standard anti-wasp measure was a jam-jar with some jam in it and a lid in the form of an inverted cone with a hole at the bottom. Wasps could get in to get the jam but found it difficult to get out.

There were usually a few angry wasps buzzing around in it plus a lot of corpses; it was definitely unaesthetic. My father decided that he could improve on this by targeting the nest itself. The problem was how to find it. Hence the visit to the chemist. In those days, one could buy almost any chemical, however lethal, provided the chemist thought he knew you and you were prepared to sign a book called the Poisons Register. I should mention that my father didn't look respectable, his chicken-farming gear would have made the average tramp think twice before accepting a swap, but he did look very like Harold Macmillan, so that may have made a difference.

Anyway, our first request this time was for potassium cyanide crystals. For younger readers, as they say, this was the poison of choice for Nazi war criminals and, in capsule form was standard issue to intelligence agents in case they were captured. The symptoms looked horribly painful but they didn't last long; it was remarkably quick to kill. The chemist asked what it was for and my father assured him that it was for wasps. "Oh, by the way," said my father, "could we have some chloroform as well?" I think the chemist may have turned a bit pale. For non-medical use so to speak, chloroform was normally associated with kidnappings and particularly violent burglaries. However my father's charm seemed to work and we got the chloroform. I don't think he could have explained how he was going to use it, as the chemist wouldn't have believed him.

Once we got home all that had to be done was to wait till evening and then capture half a dozen wasps. The next step was to put a few drops of chloroform on to cotton wool and anaesthetise the wasps. This turned out to be the tricky bit and probably why the method has never really caught on. Some of the wasps died and the ones that didn't were lively enough to make the next step rather difficult. This involved tying a piece of white cotton round the waist of the wasp, so that its flight path was visible, and one could track it back to the nest. Once again there was a critical path between too short a piece of cotton which was difficult to see and too long a piece which was too much for a somewhat drugged wasp to carry.

We did find the nest. I think one rather dishevelled wasp made its way back home, but more likely, we did what we had always done and followed them in the dusk, when they all flew back to the nest anyway. Next was the interesting bit when we tied a kitchen spoon to a six foot cane, put some of the crystals in it and tipped it on to the nest from a fairly safe distance, both the crystals and the wasps being seriously dangerous. Then a quick spray with the garden hose to activate the crystals and it was job done. Another triumph for an imaginative approach to life's problems.

There was a curious contradiction in my father's views. On the one hand he was a convinced socialist with strongly egalitarian opinions and on the other he had an almost mystical belief and even love for Lord's and the MCC. When I was about seven he took me up there, notionally to watch some cricket. Actually, I think it was a sort of blooding ceremony, to get me used to being in the Long Room of the Lord's Pavilion where I would undoubtedly be spending a lot of time once I started playing cricket for England. So it was all part of the master plan.

That day in the Long Room there were various members watching the cricket, some of them rather eminent, to whom I was introduced without any mention of my prospects as a future England player. There was also a man who had captained England not many years previously, who showed all the symptoms of what they called in his obituary 'his unfailing conviviality' and which was already showing signs of killing him. Even I was shocked.

What now surprises me about my father was his tolerance of and support for an institution which resolutely maintained a distinction between amateurs and professionals - no other cricketing country had it. Professionals (anyone who was paid to play the game) could not be members of the MCC, could not therefore enter the pavilion at Lord's and, therefore, walked out to bat from a side entrance to the pavilion, this regardless of whether they were representing England or one of the counties. It didn't apply to overseas players. On the score card professionals appeared as 'Mr' while the amateurs were 'Esquire.'

The distinction was enshrined in an old-established fixture - Gentlemen v Players. As it was virtually a trial for selecting the England team, there was still quite a lot of enthusiasm for it though the Players normally won, mainly because there was a shortage of amateur bowlers.

There was another side to the coin. A number of counties, especially Yorkshire, were reluctant to have professional captains and would recruit an amateur sufficiently competent not be an embarrassment. There was a friend of my father's who had been such a captain. He had won a cricket 'blue' at Cambridge and then captained Yorkshire for a couple of years. He had then lost the sight of one eye in an accident playing squash; with one eye he could no longer play first class cricket so now it was a question of earning his living, as the family money had more or less been used up in his cricketing days. Teaching was the obvious solution but his Cambridge degree had left him singularly ill -educated and there was nothing he could teach except games; as a pure games coach he would no longer be an amateur – there would be no more appearing in the pavilion or the Members enclosures at Headingly or Lord's. Perhaps even worse, his status would be diminished within any school he was employed at, and so presumably would his salary.

There were occasionally other sources of revenue; I discovered that the father of a boy I knew, had offered him fifty pounds to help him (the father) to become a member of the MCC. He was a brewer (nothing to do with the Brakespeares) so may have felt he needed a bit of help. I doubt if even the MCC would have held being a brewer against him.

This friend (he was called David Burton) used to come and stay with us and coach me but this was hardly a way of earning a living. All the years I knew him it was one long struggle with diminishing success. The problem, and it sounds ungrateful to say it , was he wasn't even intelligent enough to coach very well.

Once I started living in London, both my hobbies were an inducement to go down to Crossways at the week-ends and in any case, as my parents got older, I became increasingly involved in helping out with jobs round the house. The chickens had now gone but there was still an orchard to tend. One of my father's more eccentric projects was keeping down the grass in the orchard with guinea pigs. These were not the ornamental sort that turn up in shows, but basic albino pigs, mostly smooth-haired and boring, and endowed with an unfathomable ability to escape from their pens. When the cry went up, it was a three line whip to try and get them back. It even included my grandmother who, though very static, could be parked strategically to block their escape.

Eventually, my father got fed up with this and abandoned the guinea pigs in favour of equipping me with an 'Allen Cutter'. This had an unnerving resemblance to the motorised plough which had blighted my wartime childhood. It wasn't as lethal, although one could do a lot of harm to an apple tree with it. It was also very noisy and extremely hard work.

In 1954 I left St John's Wood for Kensington. I moved to a bed-sit on the first floor of a house in Inkerman Terrace, Allen St. and I stayed there happily for four years. My cooker was on the top floor landing and there was a bedroom up there as well. An Oriel friend, Chris Bell, lived there for most of the time and we got on well.

Down in the basement lived Madame Bourg. She was pleasant and friendly enough but all we wanted to talk about was her time in the French Resistance and that was strictly off limits. The owner Bill Collier lived on the ground floor and we didn't have a lot to say to each other but I do remember him agonising about whether to accept the landlords' offer to convert the lease on the house into freehold for a payment of £5000. Rather meanly, I advised him against the deal – I really didn't like him very much – but he probably worked that out for himself.

Round the corner lived David Corcos, a friend from Oriel days. He always had a taste for rather unusual entertaining – for one dinner party he prepared a dish of snipe. This was definitely a first time for the rest of us, not least because the snipe arrived from the butcher with their heads twisted round and their long beaks pushed through their breasts; except for one of them which seemed to have a raptor's beak; it wasn't very big; was it a golden eagle chick which had got in by mistake?

A game he played resulted in a unique display of oenophilic ability on my part. For his birthday, David would produce four or five different wines, all decanted and unlabelled. The game was to be able to identify them correctly. On this occasion David was clearly rather excited and on edge over one of the wines. Even I could tell that it was a huge wine and pretty certainly claret rather than burgundy. Could he have actually gone for a 'first growth'? If he had, it would almost certainly be Ch Latour, there was simply more of it around than the other first growths.

What year? Well in the nineteen-fifties, it probably had to be pre-war and there were not too many of them around and only the best would have survived. The best of the best was 1929. So I went for it and milked the situation for what I could with drawn out suspense, "I think that could only be Latour 1929." Pissed off rather than impressed was I think the mot juste. After that, normal service was resumed with a marked inability to distinguish Rhone from Chianti.

I never had very cordial relations with my landlords but resentment stopped short of an attempt to kill or maim me. On the other hand David's landlady was caught 'in flagrante delicto' putting butter on the front doorstep. It was a steep step leading pretty much straight onto the street. I suppose attempted murder might have carried quite a heavy sentence, not to mention a lot of unseemly laughter in court. In fact I think all she got was a good talking – to from the police.

One aspect of coming down from Oxford gradually came home to me, the fact that while one kept in touch more or less successfully with one's close friends there were a lot of people at Oriel who were outside that group but whose absence left a noticeable gap. One such was Eric Mortis whom I never knew well except by reputation. He was a big guy with a soft dreamy smile who used to spend the Long (summer) Vacation working as a deck hand on North Sea trawlers.

One year he decided to vary this by taking his motor bike off to the Isle of Man to compete in the TT race. Unfortunately he came off the bike at something over a hundred miles an hour and severely damaged the ligaments in his shoulder. This was where the peculiar structure of Oxford Medicine (Eric may even have been reading medicine himself) came into play. On the one hand there was the Ratcliffe Infirmary with all the resources of the NHS at its disposal and on the other we had at Oriel a Professor of Medicine, head of the Faculty of Medicine, who doubled as the college doctor and nurse.

There was disagreement between the two bodies as to how to treat the shoulder; one school preferred a conventional sling, the other a much more elaborate contraption which held his arm pointing upwards; rather like the Statue of Liberty. A statesmanlike compromise was reached whereby he used the treatments on alternate days. It seemed to take a long time to heal.

Eric made the best of the situation by taking up racing Morgan three – wheelers. Though not as fast as the motor bike they were regarded as considerably more dangerous and as such eminently satisfactory. Because it was Eric's left shoulder which was damaged, he had to use his right hand to change gear, while steadying the steering wheel with his knee, all this while racing. I did miss Eric.

On the other hand I had an unexpected encounter with someone whom I knew very slightly at Oriel. One evening in really thick fog, I was on my way home, had just come out of

Earl's Court tube station and was peering around trying to get my bearings, when a figure loomed out of the fog and asked me for a light. In Earl's Court at that time of night, the convention was that this request had nothing to do with smoking. Mutual recognition was followed on his part by something like panic and before I could put some polite enquiry like, "Do you often come here?" he had disappeared into the fog for ever.

I did make two friends in Lloyd's, and they were both men who had shared my past although we hadn't known each other at the time. Bill Mitchell had been at Oxford (at Merton, just round the corner from Oriel) and now was working like me in an underwriting box. Unlike me, he was a proper cricketer and had played for the University as a leg-spin bowler in successive years. I believe he got both May and Sheppard's wickets, both subsequently successful test cricketers. Bill had also scored a fifty in trying circumstances; they usually were in the Lord's game.

We used to have lunch together virtually every day – the arrangement went on for an incredible fifteen years – I find it difficult now to work out quite why. We were sometimes joined by David Whately; he had been at Downside with me, in fact had been injured in the plane crash – he claimed to receive a pension of fifteen pounds a year from the Treasury, but this might have been an exaggeration; however he had been in a different house and reading different subjects so we had barely met at school. He was now a broker in a small firm at Lloyd's of which he became managing director.

I suppose these lunches provided some entertainment in a rather bleak existence and there was always Lloyd's gossip to exchange.

CHAPTER 14

Granny and Jack 1930/58

While I was living as a bachelor in London, I saw far more of Granny and Uncle Jack than I had ever done before. Fairly regularly Granny would invite me to dinner (roast shoulder of lamb with all the trimmings and caramel custard); Jack and I were required to finish it up. By this time, Jack was in his sixties and showing considerable signs of wear.

My father and his brother Jack, 1903

He must have been about three or four when his mother walked out on his father and, since then, they had spent a several years in what could unkindly be called couch surfing round English stately homes, before being sent on trips to find work, first in America then in Rhodesia; both had proved disastrous.

By modern standards, he would probably be regarded as having had very little chance. In those days, the question of his needs as a youngster would probably not even have been considered and by the time I was born he was a complete mess. This was the era of the great slump and recession so there was a shortage of jobs for men with a drink problem and only one foot. Jack turns up regularly in family photographs taken in Switzerland where my parents were living, so I imagine he can't have had a job. Another problem for Jack was not so much finding as keeping accommodation in London.

During his time in Africa he had acquired the ability to give a realistic rendering of the night cries of animals on the veldt. After a drink or two it was difficult to stop him, especially when he had reached the climax – the sound of lion eating a wildebeest. This went down badly in shared accommodation.

Another problem was his physical instability caused by having only one foot. Standing by him one had to be alert in case a sudden lurch might cause him to stamp down on one with his metal foot. He had also been known to strip all the uprights out of a staircase and to demolish a chair at one sitting so to speak.

Gradually, he and Granny had drifted into a situation where they lived together and Jack tried to make some money as best he could. He tried journalism; breeding Angora rabbits came into the story at one point. I don't think any of his projects were remotely successful. They rented houses in the country and Granny did what she was best at – socialising. This generally ended in some disaster connected with Jack's drinking. My father used to get letters outlining the crisis and always ending "Well, that's one place we shan't be able to go to again."

There was no doubt Jack was an alcoholic, perhaps that he had also become highly sensitised to drink. Many years later, not very long before she died, Granny and Jack were sharing a flat in west London a mile or so from where I was living in Kensington. I got a call from her one evening, "Jack's in his room making a dreadful noise and I'm scared if he does come out, he may hurt me". Granny was tiny and bent double, nearly ninety; it wouldn't have taken much, just a clumsy fall. I went round; Jack was still in his room shouting and occasionally banging, so I took the line of least resistance and sat it out with Granny in her room.

She started to tell me stories of her youth, the memories of an Edwardian socialite. There were accounts of house parties at Blenheim, of days racing at the Curragh and the story of the heir to her family brewery (Meux) who married a prostitute (Granny was not one to mince words); this lady sent him off on board the family yacht, with an adequate load of champagne and instructions to the captain only to return him feet foremost.

There was one story I particularly liked, relating to far more recent history. Jack had been out on a prodigious blind and feeling the need to ameliorate the stress of his return had headed for Covent Garden. He turned up at their flat in a taxi and when Granny opened the door she found him, rather like Bottom the Weaver, sound asleep embowered in hundreds of roses.

Rather pathetically, there were other stories of having to go on a search round the places where he used to drink, in the hope of finding him.

After the mayhem, we discovered all this noise had been

caused by his consuming one tiny bottle of barley wine, no more than 330cl.

There had been something similar roughly, twenty years before. After a particularly bad patch, there had been a concerted family effort to dry Jack out. One of my mother's brothers, Walter, had a farm two miles away from Crossways. Being chronically strapped for cash, he agreed to take Jack as a paying guest. As it happened a friend of mine and I (we were about ten) were staying at the farm when Jack arrived.

The scheme was carefully set up. Walter could not afford to have any drink on the premises. The nearest pub was two miles away, well out of Jack's walking range and one way or another his luggage had been checked for bottles.

The following morning at breakfast my friend and I thought Jack was behaving rather oddly. Everyone else knew exactly what the problem was. But how had he managed it? The visit terminated shortly afterwards, there didn't seem a lot of point. Debate on how it came about continued for a long time afterwards, well into the period when I could contribute my own expert view. It was never properly solved, I suppose you could say his secret died with him. Later on my mother was convinced it was caused by drugs, but there wasn't any real evidence for that.

There was a similarity between the life of my father's family and astro-physics. After the 'big bang' of my grandparents' separation, my grandmother and her two children were held in orbit round each other even though the relationship was hardly a happy one. My father went to considerable lengths to avoid having anything to do with his mother – short of breaking off the relationship altogether. The same went for his relations with Jack, while Jack and his mother got drawn ever closer into mutual dependence and resentment. This took the form of formal politeness corrupted by point scoring. I can still remember their dreadful visits to Crossways when every decision was preceded by a litany of "You say" "No, you say". The rules of the game decreed that the one who cracked first and actually said what they wanted to do, was guilty of selfishness and had therefore lost. The only way to win was to persuade the other person to say they wanted what you had chosen. It was hard to see how they kept it going, as they did, for thirty years.

Granny was always fond of me, perhaps only out of duty as I was her only grandchild. I grew to appreciate her more as I matured. She was incredibly tough, extremely narrow minded and had a gambling streak, which I suppose went with her background. I have a horse-shoe mounted as a paper-holder which belonged to a filly called 'Little Eva' which won the Lincoln handicap, the first classic of the season, in 1901. Two army captains are shown as the owners; that was because Granny was forced to sell the horse on the evening before the race to pay her gambling debts.

Another thing I enjoyed was her pronunciation – fashionable Edwardian. Gels for girls of course but also 'O' pronounced as the first 'O' in onion. Thus one had Cuvent Garden, Ascut, Brumpton; I don't think monastery ever fitted into the scheme of things.

Her family background remained somewhat obscure. I have a portrait of her grandfather, looking tightlipped and Victorian, although I suppose he would have been earlier than that. According to family legend, his sister married the Duke of Sutherland – not the most popular man in Scottish history – but my limited research suggests otherwise.

The lady whom Granny wrongly referred to as a prostitute is much better documented. Her name was Lady Valerie Meux and there is a long article about her in Wikipedia. She had certainly been an actress and was not accepted socially by the family. Her husband, Sir Henry, had died aged forty four. So, allowing for Granny's generally acerbic tone, her version squared quite well with the official one.

What Granny didn't mention to me was Lady Valerie's subsequent history. After her husband's death, she had splashed her money around (there seemed to be plenty of it) and entertained in posh, though perhaps not the most respectable, society – Edward VII and Winston Churchill are mentioned. She bought Temple Gate, one of the gates of the City of London built by Wren, as an ornament for her house in the country. Finally she became friends with a General and helped out the British Army in the Boer war by supplying it with six naval field guns which she had purchased herself. And she had been painted three times by James McNeil Whistler, on the last occasion threatening to get another painter to finish the portrait and falling out with Whistler badly enough for him to destroy it.

Altogether, she would be an ornament to many a family tree and certainly a great deal of fun. The difficulty I have experienced is tracing the connection with Granny which is more tenuous.

After her marriage, Granny was obviously Mrs Hussey, so one has to look before 1895. She certainly turns up on her birth and marriage certificates as Meux -Smith, as does her father, but in the family tree she is shown as Mabel Smith; hyphenation was endemic among the Smiths in Edwardian times so she may possibly not have been a relation of the Meux family even by marriage. However, the story as told by Granny seemed quite near home – she certainly regarded the Meux brewery as belonging to her family and it would explain where her money came from.

My paternal grandmother 1916

During the war, Jack served as a captain in the Army Pay corps. In view of his age, and particularly his disability, this was the most that could have been expected of him. The money must have been welcome although I imagine the cost of his habits would have come out in front. There was one curious episode. Presumably to boost morale, although it seems incomprehensible, Harrods decided to display a photograph of Jack in service dress. Far from projecting the lean and hungry look of, say, Field Marshall Montgomery, the effect was that of a fat cat in its natural habitat – Harrods shop window. Perhaps they were forecasting a shift towards conscripting the middle aged but the picture of Jack in service dress can't have done a lot for the morale of those doing the actual fighting.

During the war, Jack and Granny lived an itinerant existence in a series of flats in Dolphin Square. Reputedly the largest block of flats in Europe before the war, it had a certain cachet and features often in the Poirot TV series. Granny had a number of acquaintances living there. They seemed to be endlessly on the move. Whereas Granny, having put up with Sinn Fein, saw no reason to pay any attention to German bombers (filthy foreigners), others were less resolute, and were only too keen to keep their flat occupied and the lease kept in place – by someone else. The building was bombed but not with serious consequences; it was probably heavily over-engineered.

By the end of the war, inflation and extravagance were eating into Granny's capital and income and the owners of the flats came home. From then on, she and Jack trekked inexorably westward. As a last vestige of her socialite days,

Kensington needed to appear in the address, but it's a big area and that was none too difficult. I tried once to tempt her with a move in the direction of Baker Street but "Oh no dear, we couldn't possibly – it's so cold north of the Park." In those days, the flats she rented seemed mostly to be owned by ladies, perhaps widows, of a certain age with whom Granny carried on guerrilla warfare. I remember one occasion when the landlady's cat had been sick on the hall carpet, Granny made a tactical delay before telling her, to make sure the cleaning lady had left and the landlady would have to clean it up herself.

Shopping was mainly by account at Harrods. She tested the system fairly thoroughly; orders were normally placed between midnight and three in the morning when Granny was at her sparkiest and frequently were for one loaf of bread to be delivered to, say, West Kensington. Someone at Harrods once retaliated and had two dozen delivered.

Multi-culturalism was not Granny's thing. Indeed, even by the standards of the time, her opinions were spectacular. During the Hungarian revolt, which at the time was being brutally put down by Russian tanks, she said to me, "Of course one's terribly sorry for the poor Hungarians, but what can you expect with all these foreigners everywhere." She had to modify that opinion when on one of her forays by bus, (it started suddenly as she was getting on – they would never give her the time she needed) she fell off backwards, would probably have been killed, but was caught in mid-air by a large Jamaican. He was incredibly kind and polite to her and wiped out at a stroke nearly ninety years of colour prejudice, greatly to the amusement of the family who thought it was high time that in this respect at least, she got her come-uppance.

At the same time, she was quite even-handed in her prejudices. When we became engaged, I took Susan to meet her –it was only a few months before Granny died. I got a letter from her to this effect, I can almost hear her speaking, "It was so nice to meet Miss Rountree, I'm sure you will be very happy together. Gels being what they are nowadays, God knows what you might have brought home with you."

During the war I was sent up to London at intervals to spend the day with her. She was genuinely fond of me, and my father was genuinely keen on any arrangement which absolved him from having anything to do with her. She was tiny and bent double and would cross the London streets by picking a moment, rather arbitrarily, and charging. My last instructions before leaving home were always, "Remember, if you don't think it's safe, let her go!" We usually went to the cinema – the latest Disney cartoon. Once we went to Lord's and it was a disaster; she really didn't know how to behave there and kept fidgeting to leave early.

When Granny died in 1958, aged almost ninety, there was a marked shortage of friends and relations at the funeral. She was buried in Chiswick cemetery on a bitterly cold spring day. My recollection is that Jack and I were the only mourners. I don't think I have ever seen anyone so completely shattered as Jack was that day. Their life together had, in some respects, been dreadful, but the future was worse.

It would have been better had there been any prospect of his marrying. He had on occasion entertained, if that is the right word, my aunt Audrey. She was exceptionally timid and retiring and any relationship with Jack had foundered on an occasion in a restaurant in Oxford, when he had got rather drunk and demanded special treatment on the grounds he was the editor of The Manchester Guardian. Audrey was never strong on sense of humour.

There was someone, the name has gone, whom he remained on terms with for a very long time and indeed left her his property, such as it was. She was mentioned, but never met and must have been singularly patient. As my father said, "He showed her all the usual signs of affection, like being sick on her doorstep."

His last years were spent living at the Stuart Hotel on Richmond Hill. We lived in Kingston, the other side of Richmond Park, so intermittently we had family lunches. They were fraught affairs. Jack didn't drink at the meal but he clearly had had to stiffen his resolve before meeting us. There really wasn't a great deal to talk about and family history was strictly off the agenda.

Then he was taken into Putney Hospital with cancer of the bladder. The surgeon asked to speak to me and explained that surgery was theoretically possible but that quality of life would be severely diminished, "How would your uncle be likely to cope?" Unspoken between us was the fact that Jack was so petrified of dying that anything, anything would have been preferred. I didn't feel very grateful to the surgeon then and I don't now. In the end I said he was having quite a lot of difficulty coping as it was, which was true and I believe it was the right answer.

His was a sad story. He was fond of me and, certainly as a child, I enjoyed his company. He went to some lengths to make a friendship, we even played squash a few times which must have been a severe test on his damaged leg but, at the end of it all, he had become so brain damaged and socially inept that it was hard work to put up with his company. It wasn't as though he was stupid, he had once been very good with figures. What an epitaph.

CHAPTER 15

Getting Married and Philbeach Gardens 1957/62

Early in1957, Bill Mitchell and I were trying to find a couple of seats on the Ingham ski-train at Victoria. Victoria Station is not normally regarded as one of those crucial 'forks in the road,' more part of the everyday rat run for people trying to get from A to B with the least possible fuss; not a place then for life-changing decisions. This time we found two seats and prepared for the long haul to Austria.

There were two girls sitting opposite called Judy and Susan. One of the objects of the ski-train, apart of course from getting one somewhere near the ski slopes, was for everyone to get to know each other, in some cases extremely well. So we were all set to chat and make friends.

With my instinct for lost causes, I quite fancied Judy. It wasn't reciprocated and didn't last more than ten minutes. I discovered later that I had been at Oriel with her brother and he hadn't liked me much either, so I expect it ran in the family. We were all going to Solden in Austria for a fortnight's skiing.

Both Bill and I had skied before, so we were put in a higher class than Judy and Susan which was probably just as well. Susan had some claims to be the worst skier in England, not because she fell over a lot, we all did that, but because she was quite incapable of getting up unaided. It wasn't attention seeking – that wasn't her style, but genuine incapacity. It's hard to overstate how irritating this could be and I never could make out how she had come to be on a skiing holiday in the first place.

It turned out that our choice of seats had been more significant than I had realised. When we finished the holiday, we made the usual exchange of addresses and I discovered that Susan lived round the corner from me in Cornwall Gardens, South Kensington. Going skiing with her again was clearly not an option but even I had begun to realise that there were other things in life and off the slopes we had got on really well; besides I had damaged my shoulder quite severely on the last day in Solden which helped settle the question. I wouldn't be going skiing for a year or so.

Susan lived with her parents in a large ground floor and basement flat. Family life was fairly fraught. Susan's father, Gilbert Rountree, would have been a good stand-in for 'Rumpole of the Bailey' – he was a clever criminal law junior; his career had been held back by the war so he was on the old side for a Junior, and he survived on a diet of gin and cigarettes.

It was his home life in which the similarity really showed. He was completely hopeless with money and the system didn't help. Barristers' fees were collected, or not, by the chamber's clerk, an important figure something like a Company Sergeant-Major in the army, and they were almost invariably paid late. But the clerk was also responsible for the allocation of briefs so it paid not to upset him by too aggressive an attitude over fees owed, if you wanted a share of the better briefs. A certain forbearance was necessary.

This forbearance didn't extend to Gilbert's wife who, with some justice, suspected Gilbert of dissipating his earnings in the pub on the way home. He was prone to expensively flamboyant gestures in congenial company, hence a lot of screaming and shouting when he got back. In the midst of all this, Susan kept her head down, kept well clear of her mother and survived on her own. I ventured into this maelstrom rather cautiously.

It was suggested that Susan's mother, Pixie, as she was always known, was in awe of me. If true, this was something quite unlike anything I had ever experienced before and didn't know how to cope with. I thought that perhaps it was a misunderstanding of my rather nervous expression, which she took for lofty disapproval. At all events it seemed to work in my favour and gradually the Rountrees got used to my being around.

Susan had a scooter, a Lambretta, which took us everywhere, including on one occasion up the steps of one of the houses in Cornwall Gardens, and could be parked almost anywhere. We even went down to see my parents in Henley. It was very hard work getting there, as the lights on the Lambretta were lamentable but the venture was well received. I suppose a lot of people regard their parents as so peculiar that they can't imagine any girlfriend getting on with them. I needn't have worried.

One day that autumn, Susan took herself off to stay in a pub near Arundel. I wasn't sure what this was about, other than a longer step than usual away from her mother. I enquired if I could come down and join her and that was apparently all right; so I did. By the end of the week-end we were going to get married, so that really was all right.

This meant a change in my social position; I got officially asked to dinner parties, which wasn't an unmixed blessing. For a start Pixie, my future mother-in-law, took great pride in her reputation as a cook – not a view which Susan and I shared, although it was backed up by her having made an omelette in the presence of King George the Fifth at a demonstration at the Ideal Home Exhibition.

On top of this, the other guests tended to be barristers, professionally used to holding the floor unchallenged. I missed one of the finer moments when a friend from Gilbert's Air Force days during the war, whom he hadn't seen for some time, turned out to have come up before one of the other guests for a particularly bad 'Drunk in Charge' and had been sent to jail. On the whole I wasn't required to say very much at these dinners or to comment on the wine, which tended to be execrable.

There was one dinner party with the proprietors of the News of the World. All I remember of that was the size of the rocks that the lady was wearing.

There was also some socialising among my friends. I could manage dinner parties at Inkerman Terrace cooking on the Baby Belling on the top floor. Chris Bell was often there and friends from Oxford days, including Stella, used to turn up. Whately always referred to Susan as 'poor Miss Rountree' which I understood as a reference to 'Portrait of a Lady'; as if I should be so lucky; Susan definitely wasn't an heiress, however much I resembled Gilbert Osmond.

We were married on the fifth of July 1958. The reception was at my parents in law's flat and there were about eighty people there, which was probably fifty too many. Whately was our best man and managed to restrain himself from referring to Susan as poor Miss Rountree. Fifty years on, Susan and I discovered an account book kept by my mother -in-law detailing all debits and credits relating to the wedding. What surprised us most was the preponderance of quite un-presenty items, useful things for the kitchen and so on, and how many of them we had managed to keep and use.

Guess what? 1958 (the day after Independence Day!)

We were not off to France until the following day and for some reason had chosen to go to Covent Garden – Aida – it was not my favourite opera and not totally encouraging for a newly married couple. We skipped the bit where the lovers were buried alive, drifted back to the reception – everyone had gone to another party, so we finished up back at our new flat and, not for the last time in our married life, went early to bed.

The Lambretta was an integral part of our honeymoon plans. We had arranged in advance for it to be put on the train for collection in Paris. Apart from the weight of our luggage on the back, which lifted the front wheel in the air, a violent thunderstorm and the fact that the top suitcase turned out not to be waterproof, we made it successfully – albeit rather uncertainly – from the Gare du Nord to the Gare de Lyon.

We collected the scooter off the train at Lyon and drove down the Route Napoleon over the Alps. The most noticeable feature of the trip was that going up the passes, we were using so much fuel that, being a two-stroke, the sparking plug oiled up and we had to stop and clean it every few miles, while coming down we were using so little that the cylinder got no lubrication at all. There was also one part which was so steep that Susan had to get off and walk, while I drove on. I am still surprised at this.

We reached Cannes and found a pleasant hotel at Theoule-sur-Mer about five miles out. To get to the beach, one had to cross a main road but we weren't in the mood to be fussy and in any case were prepared to move on. Travelling on the scooter cost practically nothing. So we went on; St Raphael, which we took for a pretty little village – until we saw the rest of it , St Tropez where we bought a wall lamp, ill-advised in the long run, and where a rat came out on the harbour wall and ate some scraps from our picnic. Finally, we stayed at Frejus with a nice lady who fed us with unlimited peaches which she grew commercially. A few years later, I wondered if she had survived the bursting of the dam. It seemed unlikely to judge from the position of her house.

That was pretty much the end of our honeymoon. All we had to do was to get home. We had all the tickets we needed and a fullish tank of petrol. What we lacked was money – I had a pocketful of nothing much and Susan had nothing at all.

We got on the train to Paris in rather sombre mood as our hopes rested entirely on a pamphlet I had casually picked up in London showing the address of Barclays in Paris. You could tell where it was, when we got to the right area, by the queue of depressed looking punters all on the same mission. God bless Barclays! All you needed was a Barclays' cheque book and they would give you five pounds.

It may not seem much, it sounds better as seven thousand francs, which in those days was equivalent, but with it we got a room for the night at a pleasant hotel close to the Opera, a snack lunch somewhere nearby and dinner in Montmartre (I had osso bucco). There were even a few centimes over for a coffee at the station in the morning as we made for home and settled down to married life.

We had bought the fag-end of a lease of a flat in Earl's Court – Philbeach Gardens. It was only for two years or so, but we hoped my finances would look up as I had just become a member of Lloyd's, with some hope of making some money and by that time we would be able to buy somewhere to live. It had been a large house, now converted into four comfortable flats.

One day, I was leaving the front door when I met a man wearing an Oriel Games tie visiting the ground floor basement flat. Didn't I know the Coopers? Well, not at that time; so he took me in to meet them. Dan Cooper had gone up to Oriel the term after I came down. He had met Pat at Oxford so they had been married for some time by then. He was by a long way the largest 'larger than life' character I ever met.

It's difficult to know where to start with the Coopers. They occupied a huge part of our life, always fun and sometimes trouble as well. We were also friendly with another couple living above us; they had just been married, but for them it was a second shot so they were older – and posher. Peter, the husband, used to have a copy of the Times delivered each morning. Dan used to steal it and retire to the bath to read it. This caused a lot of grief from which we had to steer well clear and which gave me a taste of what life with Dan was going to be like.

Dan's mother was Robert Graves' sister. It's probably fair to say that brother and sister disliked each other intensely. There is a novel by Robert Graves, 'Antigua Penny Puce', about a squabble between brother and sister over an inheritance, which 'the Doc,' Dan's mother, found especially irritating. Funnily enough, the sister in the story is incredibly devious while the son is frank, open and honest.

The Doc had been married to someone called Cooper. They had divorced and he had taken his new wife's name – Tuthill. He was always known as Tuthill in the family. I met him once; he was ill in bed in Dan and Pat's flat. He did appear completely barmy.

At about this time, Dan and a friend had somehow acquired a house in Spain which they decided to rent out for holiday lets. It worked so well that they decided to turn it into a business, rent properties themselves and sublet them for holidays. And so Rentavilla was born.

I have no excuse for including this as part of the story, except it all happened while we were still at Philbeach Gardens. The critical period of each year for Rentavilla was when they were, in effect, matching the incoming bookings with the properties they were taking on. This year, Dan had been skiing, something he was not designed to do, being six foot three and heavily built, and had broken his thigh. He took his eye off the ball; there were recriminations with Doug, his partner, and the cash flow took a serious hit. Tuthill came to the rescue and then promptly sacked Dan and Doug. Doug bided his time, waited for the company to come to grief under Tuthill's management, which happened surprisingly quickly, then bought it back at famine prices; Dan and his family went off to New York.

One more story. It all happened about thirteen years later, when Dan and Pat were living in Mont Saxonnez, about ten miles from Geneva. We were all there on holiday and it happened to be our daughter Catherine's birthday. Dinner out at one of the villages was mooted. Pat suggested one they knew, Dan wanted to go to another where there was a fireworks display; we sided with Pat. It was arranged to meet Dan at the United Nations where he was employed as a translator.

We had a large Volvo and, come the evening, managed to fit three adults, three Hussey children and three or four Cooper children into it. Fortunately some of them were quite little. At the border, the Swiss guard started counting, then gave up and waved us through.

The first sign of problems ahead was Dan's Ford parked on the immaculate Geneva green sward by the lake with a large sign saying 'en panne'.

The only solution was to buy another car. Dan found an elderly Peugeot which he bought for 750 francs. The best thing about it was a half-bottle of vodka in the glove compartment and there was a further problem; in Switzerland, number plates went with the owner, not the car, so now we had one set of number plates and two cars, one for driving and one parked ludicrously publicly in one of the most pristine parts of Geneva.

Clearly the only answer was to share out the number plates, so leaving one number plate on the Ford, facing the direction we optimistically hoped the police would approach it from, we put the other on the front of the Peugeot. We had three frontier crossings to make, Switzerland to France and back again, and we reasoned that by the time any guard spotted there was no plate on the back, we would be through the crossing.

Surprisingly, we got through the border posts without any trouble but we arrived at dinner rather late and after one course, Dan suddenly disappeared, presumably in search of fireworks, and no one saw him again for three or four days. Pat and I did go looking for him and found traces of where he had been – at a village wedding and so on.

Back to 1960. Our lease was coming to an end and we had to find somewhere to live. It was just as difficult then as now, but the figures, even allowing for inflation, were hundreds or even thousands of times smaller. It was the time of Roy Brooks' property advertisements; the best known was 'spare room suitable for a nimble dwarf' giving a misleading impression of total frankness, but they made a welcome change from the general run of estate agents prose and were often less misleading. One we looked at was described as having 'a convenient train service.' It didn't mention that the line ran about ten foot away from the house.

Eventually, we lit on one we could afford. 'Elegant Neo-Palladian Victorian terrace house in quiet cul-de-sac £1200.' It is completely unbelievable today. Then we were merely wary. It was in Chancellors St, just back from the river at Hammersmith. It was certainly in a cul-de-sac; quiet was more debatable; there was a large primary school just behind it, so during the day this didn't apply. Then if it rained, which it sometimes did, the pumping house next door (we were the last house in the terrace) was spectacularly noisy. Then again, Neo-Palladian? Well, it did have an entablature but the street was so narrow one couldn't possibly see it.

They didn't mention that there was no bathroom and that the only loo was outside in the yard. What there was a lot of, was dry rot. Susan went round to the council to talk to them about borrowing money to do it up. The man at the council was avuncular, he said, "I'm afraid you paid too much" and when I got the title deeds, I discovered that the previous owner, admittedly in 1939, had paid £100 each for six of the houses.

A certain amount of damage had occurred since then. During the war, a doodle bomb had landed a short distance away and the whole terrace had lurched sideways. One could easily see the front door was rhomboid and on the day we moved in, the council engineer served a 'dangerous structure' notice to the effect that our chimney stack was pulling the whole terrace over.

We spent nearly three years there but most of the first year was spent building and repairing. In those days, everyone in our position hoped for the gentrification of their street and a sudden surge in value; we inched imperceptibly in that direction. One family in the street owned a Vauxhall saloon in which they used to spend the evening listening to the car radio, the house itself being unreconstructed. Two doors along from us was a schoolmaster. He was unbelievably camp and his house was amazing, it could have been decorated by Huysmans. We had supper with him and asked him back but I'm afraid we couldn't live up to his expectations, which was a shame.

Along from him there was a ménage a trois. A painter who would daily turn out four foot canvases of execrable quality, a sculptor working in heavy metal and a postman who presumably earned the cash to keep the ship afloat. One day there was a loud bang and a mushroom cloud formed over their house; after an interval, heads appeared out of the window looking black and shocked. It transpired that the top floor ceiling had fallen without warning, engulfing them in plaster and soot; it was a weakness in all the houses.

Across the other side of the street was a house of sinister multi-occupancy and I earned the good-will of the police by allowing them to park an observer on our flat roof. I never found out what happened over this but the other alternative to gentrification was a sudden plunge into multi-occupancy squalor, so this episode served as a warning and we decided to take the hint and move on.

CHAPTER 16

Early days in Surrey 1962/72

There's a Flanders and Swan song 'We're terribly House and Garden at No 7b, we've rediscovered the chandelier… etc.' and then the punch line 'We actually live at 7a.' We were a bit like that. Our house in Hammersmith was full of features; the most radical was forced on us. We wanted to turn the top floor into a single (fairly) large room but it was divided in two by a wall made of plaster board and studs, which the borough engineer would on no account allow us to take down. I never did discover the logic of this, it wasn't load - bearing but we settled the matter by taking down the plasterboard and leaving the studs as they were, but with a gap in the middle as a passage way. At least it improved the lighting in the room. The real problem was that there were now four of us and the house was a bit small.

The winter of 1961/2 provided additional incentive. Susan's mother had come to stay with us over Christmas. On Boxing Day, it started to snow, quite light, fine snow and it didn't stop for a couple of months. By some reckoning it was the worst winter of the century. Pixie, Susan's mother, was now widowed and at that time living in Cornwall. Her house was completely cut off by snow drifts, so she remained camped in our sitting room on the top floor, keeping warm with electric fires. The roof insulation was negligible so when I walked home in the evening, I could see the rest of the terrace with snow on the roofs and ours, at the end, with a mist rising from it.

We aimed at getting about £5000 for the house, which, taking into account the money spent on improvements, would double what we had as a deposit for the next house, with a bit to spare. There were a fair number of four-bedroom detached Victorian houses in the outer suburbs selling for £8000 or just over, so with a bit of luck we could make it.

We found an agent, advertised the Chancellor St house and had what I imagine is still the usual response at the bottom end of the market, non-stop viewing from eight o'clock onwards. We learnt a valuable lesson about selling that day; we put a lot of work into persuading people how attractive it was and it wasn't until right at the end of the day, when we were too exhausted to get involved, that we made a sale. The other lesson we learnt came from a later visit; the woman who bought it was terribly enthusiastic about our decorations 'they really sold the place to her;' by the time I came back they had all been painted over.

By contrast, buying the house in Kingston was a civilised affair; I don't think we were competing with anyone else which seems quite peculiar. It was number 22, Queens Road and its greatest advantage was that it was only a hundred yards from the gate to Richmond Park. Unlike our wreck at Hammersmith which had pretensions to neo-classical gentility, this was mid-Victorian and looked it. It had been built in1865 by a builder to live in himself and he had lavished a lot of attention on the detail. There was a bay window in front on which there was a complete fruit salad in stucco and a gate to the front garden saying, 'Clive Lodge' and 'No Hawkers or Circulars.' The day we moved in, we spotted the occupants of the flats the other side of the street inspecting us and our belongings through field glasses; it was nice to feel we hadn't entirely left the ethos of Chancellor Street behind us.

Number 22 Queens Road had leaded lights throughout, though I don't think they were original. They were completely disastrous; I don't think I have ever come across a worse idea. They were extremely draughty, excluded about a third of the light and looked terrible. I got rid of them and then, in the cause of draught exclusion, put a second door in the front of the porch. I went to some trouble to have it made to a tasteful Georgian design and it looked quite ridiculous. I see it whenever I go up to Kingston and it doesn't get any better.

D.I.Y. was all the rage and I decided to renew the plumbing and put in central heating. When I say I decided to do it, I mean exactly that – doing it myself. The plumbing was the hardest part; my first job was 'to wipe a joint.' I had to look up 'Every Man His Own Plumber' for that. The worst thing was, it was on the main supply coming in to the stopcock which was, of course, at full mains pressure; it was necessary because the mains piping was made of lead and I wanted to replace all the lead pipe in the house with copper pipe. Clearly, the mains lead pipe would have to be joined to copper pipe.

As instructed by my book, you make a paper funnel round the copper pipe and pour molten lead into the funnel until you have built up a thick collar of lead round the joint. Then you wipe it with a moleskin. If the lead is still hot enough to be malleable (and burn your fingers), wiping it makes a watertight skin over the joint. Today not many plumbers get called on to do this and the supply of moleskins is limited. It came right on the third shot and I was able to stop running out to the pavement to turn the mains on and off. I was beginning to realise that I was going to get a lot of exercise during this project.

Apart from reducing the chance of lead poisoning from the pipes, the ultimate goal was to put in a new cold water tank made of plastic. The existing one was made of lead with a framework of wood holding it together. Apart from the probability that at some point the wooden frame would cease to do its job and we would have a major flood, it seemed a good idea not to have our water supply enclosed in lead.

Always on the lookout for an opportunity to recycle, Susan persuaded a neighbour who was a sculptress to convert the cold water tank into a sculpture. It wasn't difficult, just a matter of extracting several hundredweight of lead sheeting from rather a tight spot in our attic and getting it round to our friend without buckling it. Our friend Elaine joined up the four panels successfully and produced a handsome sculpture about eight feet long by three feet high.

All that was needed now was to make a fibreglass backing to stabilise and strengthen the lead sculpture. Under her guidance, Elaine and I stippled on the fibreglass; needless to say it was raining so we had to do it under a tarpaulin. She said, "I believe this stuff is meant to turn you on." It just gave me a headache.

Mr Haggis was the name of our local builder. We and our neighbours all used him; as well as doing reasonable building work and having a competent workforce, (although according to Susan he did have a decorator permanently programmed to sing 'I'll do it my way,'), he gave good advice for nothing. It was he who told me, when I was doing the plumbing, "On no account turn off your own stop-cock. Get a key for the water-board's valve under the pavement. Then when it leaks (which it will) all you have to do is to ring them up and tell them to fix it"

He incited me to take on projects which tested my ability. His standard advice was, "no, no you don't need me for this, you do so-and-so and then I'll come and finish it off." Once he said, "I see myself as a sort of Robin Hood of the building trade. I know you can't afford a lot of work but I can usually find a way to keep your bills reasonable." Shortly afterwards I found myself trying to keep a straight face when our far more affluent neighbour was leaping up and down about Haggis' charges.

Mr Haggis had a secret vice. Most Sundays he would get up early and ride his BMW motor cycle down the M4 to Newport for a cup of coffee, then ride back to Kingston for Sunday lunch. I suppose there weren't many people on the motorways in those days. We never heard of him being booked for speeding.

My father died in February 1964, aged sixty six, about four months after we had moved into Queens Road. We sold Crossways fairly promptly and bought my mother a bungalow on one of the commons, half a mile away; not really my mother's sort of house but it had a nice garden and worked well inside. It had a thoroughly pretentious name so she called it 'Brambles' which seemed appropriate and happened to be the name of the previous owner.

There remained a problem. My parents had been married thirty seven years and during that time my mother had nursed my father from a state of being at death's door through a period when he was healthy, although chronically incapacitated, finally to a point where his body was giving out and he was likely to die at any moment.

All this time she had been chronically ill herself, sometimes with tangible symptoms, but also with psychosomatic disorders which we attributed entirely to her confined, in some ways frustrated, life. In her youth she had been athletic, riding, playing cricket with her brothers, skiing. She greatly surprised me one day when I was buying records of Beethoven's 9th conducted by Felix Weingartner, the definitive recording at the time, saying," I knew him quite well; I used to go skating with him in Switzerland. "

The worst time was the winter, as a result of operations on her nasal passages which had not had the result desired and made her vulnerable to any infection that was going round. This was not going to be any better on her own. Someone suggested, I think it was Susan, that she goes abroad and let the house to pay for the trip. This was rapidly refined into taking a sea voyage, the problem being to find a trip that would take up a large part of the winter. I managed to find just the right thing- a Yugoslav cargo ship doing a round trip – Rijeka to Japan and back.

In those days, there were far more ships doing specific voyages, not casual tramping but not on a regular 'liner' run either. They took twelve passengers; any more and they were required to have a ship's doctor. This was such a ship, belonging to the Yugoslav Government fleet. There's a picture of it, looking smart. My mother had one great advantage, she spoke fluent German which, though not necessarily the most popular language, was a good fill-in when English didn't work. By the time she got to Rijeka in the autumn, she was quite unwell but was determined to stick it out and get better. It was going to be a tough challenge for a widow of nearly seventy in poor health.

I'm not sure who the other passengers were. All we heard about was a German who was doing the same trip. Very stout, at least as depicted in my mother's cartoons, my mother christened him 'Piggy' and we got regular bulletins and cartoons depicting him. I doubt very much whether he realised that this polite and gentle old lady engaged in her artwork was actually carrying on the final campaign of the Second World War complete with propaganda cartoons. I'm not at all sure it was just a joke, I don't think she ever forgave the Germans for indirectly causing the death of her favourite brother and this was far from unusual among her generation. My favourite picture from the trip was actually a photograph of my mother with an armful of cobras, looking understandably uneasy. She had agreed to pose simply because 'Piggy' had chickened out and it was up to her to uphold the honour of the British Empire.

Gammy with friends

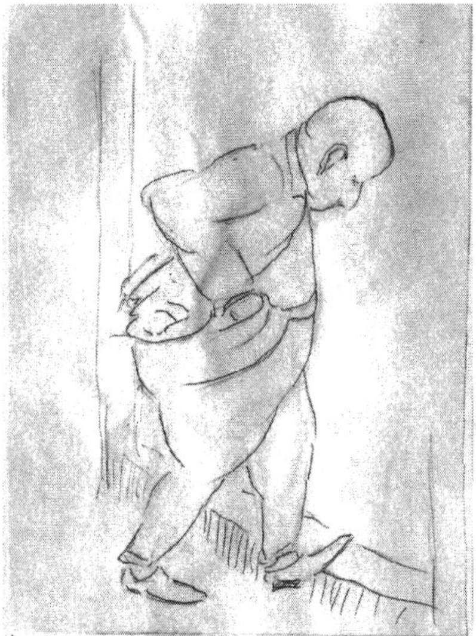

"Moment" Piggy goes for anotha bottle -

Piggy insisted on photographing the Shrine though forbidden, Nothing happened propably thought he was reincarnation of Buddha -

There had been a slight miscalculation over the trip; we hadn't noticed that Japan was in the northern hemisphere, so it came as a surprise when the first Japanese she saw were carrying skis. We got some sketches from Japan, not perhaps as much fun as some of the ones on the way out. She may have been a bit daunted by the absence of any street signs that she could read, but with the help of her fellow passengers and a lot of friendly assistance from the Japanese, she was able to go by train to Kyoto and see a lot of the country.

Eventually the ship got back to Yugoslavia – there was a coach trip to catch the plane home on which she was proposed to by a Serb or a Croat. We weren't given many details except that he had the most amazing moustache. Despite this, she turned him down, although I think she was quite flattered by the terms of the proposal.

We never managed quite to equal the success we had with this trip. Certainly we never again got such a proliferation of drawings and cartoons with such sparkling captions. There simply weren't many voyages as long as this around. My mother, by now called Gammy by my children, was always very gregarious and made two trips to Tenerife where she spent the winter cheaply and comfortably. A feature of the trips to Tenerife was that she was able to come up to the City, have lunch with me and then stroll down to London Bridge where the Aznar ship was moored. It was a very civilised system for commencing a trip abroad, only marred on a later occasion by their getting the mooring process slightly wrong and doing a fair amount of damage to London Bridge.

There was one adventurous journey to South America, a twelve passenger vessel, but quite posh – run by Holland

Amerika Line. This was once again a round trip starting in Rotterdam, through the Caribbean and the Panama Canal and down the west coast of South America and return to Rotterdam. The principal cargo involved was fishmeal, evil smelling and prone to spontaneous combustion, so not perhaps an ingredient of your average cruise, but Gammy had spent a lot of her life with farmyard smells and never complained about it.

I believe the normal system on cargo ships, certainly on this one, is for the First Officer to take command of the ship whilst it's in harbour, to supervise the loading of cargo and so on, while the Captain and Chief Engineer are free to take the day off.

As usual, Gammy's German came to her aid and when they were in port, she was invited to share a taxi with the two officers and go for long excursions round the interior of South America. This way she saw a lot of Ecuador, Peru and Chile. Apparently these drives were a great success and I got a telegram when they were coming up the channel on the way home to the effect that she had invited all the officers to come and have lunch with me in Lloyd's. It left me somewhat on edge as apart from anything else I couldn't speak either Dutch or German.

On one of her visits to Tenerife, Gammy had made friends with an American family and she was invited to go for a prolonged stay with them in Phoenix Arizona. It was a testing journey. I have a postcard of a cargo ship called the Pacific Northwest which I have been unable to trace. My belief is that she went both ways by Royal Mail so it may have been on charter. The sea journey was long, they went through the Panama Canal, but the real problem was the distance from the coast to Phoenix, roughly three hundred miles. It's a long way by Greyhound Bus.

Maybe the visit was a shade too long. I'm not sure how much Gammy enjoyed it. Her friends lived in a condominium and she was very shocked to find that out of school time, all the local kids, some of them quite young, were locked outside when their parents went to work. She formed a group and played with them to keep them entertained.

When her ship was due to arrive back in London, we went down to the King George The Fifth Dock. The country is pretty flat there and we could see the ship sailing towards us from about five or six miles away, seemingly with no water round it and looking huge in relation to its surroundings. It was a memorable experience.

When Gammy arrived home she was seriously unwell. She spent time in Kingston Hospital and afterwards, to recuperate, went to stay with her sister, got ill again and finally went to a hospital in Leamington Spa, where a surgeon who specialised in the operation removed her spleen. It seemed to help. Gammy lived for several years afterwards, having her grandchildren to stay, and occasionally coming up to Kingston for a visit. There were no more foreign cruises.

Gammy had surmounted huge obstacles to marry the man she loved and was happily married for thirty seven years. She had also managed to win round her mother-in-law who had initially shown unyielding hostility. In addition to all this, she was used to acting as a sort of lynchpin among her brothers and sisters who at times were capable of flying off in all directions.

She lived long enough to derive great pleasure from her grandchildren and you certainly couldn't call it a wasted life, though not perhaps totally fulfilled and nothing on earth would have made her complain.

CHAPTER 17

Richmond Park; horses and cars 1978/88

Like most people living in the area we had always got good value out of the park, dog walking, taking friends to the Isabella Plantation and so on. Unlike Wimbledon Common, which had its own charm but could be scary, Richmond Park was open and gave a genuine sense of peace and security.

After we had lived in Kingston about fourteen years, I was approaching fifty, getting too old for cricket and anyway needing something a bit more exciting; so I decided to take up riding. It had all started nearly twenty years before; we had been on holiday in Cornwall, staying with family friends in Port Isaac, when we saw a sign advertising horses to be hired out for hacking. Susan had ridden before, had owned her own pony as a child; it had passed me by completely though there was plenty of it in my genes.

We followed the sign, found an old woman living in a caravan in a bog, lied our heads off about our experience and were equipped with a couple of cobs. I did have a little trouble with mine, stopping, or trying to stop it, eating the hydrangeas in people's front gardens but otherwise it went well.

Back the following day and I asked for something a little bit more exciting. This was the point at which I deserved to have

Susan on horseback

got killed; she must have been quite kind because this one was perfect, or at least it went into a steady canter and stopped when asked; I thought it was the most exciting thing that had happened for some time. At that time we couldn't possibly afford to go riding in the Kingston area, but now, twenty years later we could, and were ready to start riding properly.

We began in Bushey Park. It was safe and it was fun but soon enough we wanted to buy our own horses. Susan found one - a coloured gypsy pony with a huge character but good natured and fun to ride. We stabled her at the Roehampton Stables fifty yards from the Roehampton Gate; when the Park was open, it was just a couple of miles from our house. The stables played a big part in our lives for the next ten years.

I managed to achieve almost a textbook example of how not to buy a horse for myself. For a start, the girl who owned it told me to take it out of the yard for a hack (it was a different yard to ours and I had never seen it ridden); this was quite ridiculous. Lurking beneath the reasons sometimes given for a sale - owner outgrown it, going to university etc., there is often a strong desire never to see the bloody animal again; if you're buying, it's essential to see how the owner gets on with it – it's often surprising how badly that is.

To make matters worse I had arranged for Susan to meet me on her pony, bringing the dogs. This was insane. Later experience taught me that it's completely impossible to predict what will spook a horse or even just annoy it. Dogs are often not good news and on this occasion were disastrous. The mare started bucking as soon as they arrived and eventually got me off – I was extremely inexperienced.

Most horses will try at all costs to avoid treading on a fallen rider; this one didn't. At this point, my luck took on a near-miraculous turn for the better. An ambulance crew had been watching the entertainment, scooped me up almost as soon as it happened and Kingston Hospital was only half a mile away. It must have less than an hour before I was in intensive care, morosely watching a large container gradually filling with blood from a tube plugged into my chest where the lung had been punctured.

Was it the following morning? I can't believe it arrived so quickly, but at any rate it was while I was still in intensive care. The post came with a letter from my friend Peter Reid; no text just a poem: 'To a friend on falling from his horse'

Those hands which raised the beast so high
And cast thee down in agony
With fractured ribs and punctured lung
To lie the dirt and dust among,
May purpose that the Dublin Dean
And Eton socialist be seen
Themselves sour natured, to've misled
In summing up the quadruped
That noble man trust not the whims
Of so-called nobler houyhnhms
And learn though learning make him sad
Two legs are good and four legs bad.

A copy of Gulliver's Travels and Animal Farm might have been handy but I didn't really need them. I laughed so much that it sent all my sensors into spasm and there was panic in the intensive care ward.

Despite all the broken ribs it didn't hurt much but I spent three weeks in hospital; time for a full run through of the all the emotions of which boredom always came out on top.

There was a sequel to my accident; a broker friend of the syndicate casually asked when we were going to make a claim? I should explain that there is a huge influx of business in Lloyd's over the Christmas period; companies find it convenient to have their policies matching the calendar year, so from the beginning of December onwards there was complete bedlam at the underwriting box. My departure to hospital was on about the 5th. The claim arose because I was covered for accidents under a 'Key Personnel' policy and we were entitled to about £1500.

What to do with the money? It seemed a pity to pay it to the company where it would disappear for ever and I certainly didn't feel entitled, having caused everyone else a great deal of grief by being stupid enough to fall off my horse.

So we booked "The Ivy" for the evening and had a party for the underwriting staff and very good it was.

I required some rehabilitation when I came out of hospital and a girl called Juliette, whom we knew quite well and was a riding instructor, took me in hand. First step was to find a horse we could use and we lit on a cob called Solomon. Of his kind, he was perfect; he didn't go fast or jump very high but he was endlessly kind.

At first we just did flat work with simple exercises - all the stuff I should have done much more of - then we moved on to jumping. We weren't going to win any competitions, the limit was about two foot. Juliette then started introducing variations; no stirrups, no reins, arms held out sideways and finally eyes shut.

Oddly, over small jumps it's all much easier than it sounds and makes you synchronise with the horse. I did finally ask what this was intended to achieve and Juliette just giggled - "I just wondered if I could get you to do it."

Finally, I fell off without my ribs disintegrating so I felt much better and completely rehabilitated. Juliette took charge of my next attempt at buying a horse.

Twenty years later in Cornwall, I bumped into the girl who had tried to sell me the mare and I asked what had become of it. "Oh, I sold it to a man in Lloyd's; they were made for each other, you couldn't teach either of them anything." He subsequently killed himself, although the horse didn't feature in that story.

Anyway, I now owned a great big Irish horse with big feet and hairy legs called Callan. He was lovely and, being a youngster, sufficiently lively to satisfy my yearning for adventure. We always reckoned that he and Susan's pony used to wink at each other before taking off at a gallop.

Owners kept their horses at the stables and used to ride as often as they could. If you were earning enough money to afford the livery, there was a strong possibility that you wouldn't have the time to ride very often. There was virtually no turn-out, when horses are left free to roam in a paddock to rest and relax, so to get them out a bit more often it was a good idea to fix a deal with someone whereby they could ride regularly in return for an agreed fee. It had the advantage that you knew the person, had some idea of his or her ability and could probably count on their regular appearance.

Before I owned Callan, I had a sharing arrangement on an elderly thoroughbred. It worked all right but I do remember one ride. There was a spectacular thunderstorm right overhead. You are not supposed to go under a tree in a thunderstorm but sitting on a horse is not great – four legs earthing to ground with metal plates ensuring a good connection. It was like sitting on a lightning conductor. What surprised me was that Bombay (the horse) was totally unaffected; perhaps he couldn't see the lightning, I have noticed animals seem unable to see electronic flash. As for me I couldn't wait to get out of the park.

There were about thirty horses in the yard, which was owned by Bert White and his son, Nick. They were known as 'the old man' and 'young White'. They had a rather tense relation with each other and on one occasion, young White was seen chasing his father round the yard with a pitchfork. The old man had pretensions to affluence if not gentility- there were pictures of National Hunt horses which he had owned for his son to ride. They hadn't been much good, but then I don't think young White was much of a jockey.

There were two stable lads; that is to say two Irish brothers, probably in their fifties, Ted and Jack. Ted was tall and slim with a vaguely Irish looking hat; Jack was short and dark. Unlike Ted, Jack as far as I know, never told the truth. Ted could, as they say, charm the birds off the trees, whereas Jack was totally charmless. Ted was also incredibly good with horses. If your horse was being difficult about being clipped, for example, five minutes with Ted would calm it right down. The same went for most of the owners; Ted was one of nature's troubleshooters.

If you owned a horse it was a great advantage to be able to ride at least occasionally during the day so it meant that those who owned horses tended to have unusual and interesting occupations. We had a good social mix as well. There was one girl who was a successful illustrator of children's books, another who was a croupier. My sharer was Polish, reputed to be a colonel. When the revolution in Poland started, he disappeared overnight. We didn't have many youngsters. I suppose the busiest times at the yard coincided with school hours. There was one teenager called Rosie who was on the way to becoming a serious competitive rider, unlike the rest of us in the yard whom our instructor once referred to as 'his geriatric pony club.' Rosie seemed to spend quite a lot of time in the yard and I remember finding Susan and her sitting on the muck heap - once it had matured it became quite inert - presumably discussing the meaning of life.

There was a stunt man; we steered clear of him as his other occupation seemed to involve smallish parcels which were collected anonymously from the tack-room. There was an eccentric lady who never owned a horse herself, but regularly had sharing arrangements and occasionally rode round the park stark naked. She came to grief riding the stunt man's horse, an elderly thoroughbred called Biggles.

She decided one hot day to take Biggles for a paddle in Beverley Brook, a stream running through the park; it wasn't a good idea, the sides were steep, Biggles slipped and cut himself. The stunt man demanded she paid the vet's bills, then, sensing a commercial opportunity claimed that Biggles had died and that she was responsible. This would have cost a few hundred pounds at least, with the advantage for the stunt man of not having to share the money with the vet. Fortunately Ted's relations came to the rescue and established that Biggles had been sold and was living in Ireland.

There were two girls working in the yard, both very good fun. Yvonne had been married to a vicar who kept snakes as a hobby. Eventually, the snakes had come between them and she had left him. She had had a fling with Ted, which was more or less entry level, but had got over that and was on her own. Fiona, the other girl, lived round the corner from us. She had had a baby at fifteen and lived with her very unsatisfactory husband.

She was amazing, so full of energy, and we eventually helped her to get a job in the graphics department of Kew Gardens. Along the way, one weekend she borrowed our springer spaniel Wellington and took him off to Guildford dog show where he won Best in Class. He was very handsome but smelt appallingly from incurable 'spaniel ears.' The judge's sense of smell must have completely atrophied.

The farrier is one of the most important people in any yard; he is the one who literally keeps the show on the road. With thirty horses in the yard, our man 'Bob' used to come once a fortnight and usually had half a dozen horses to shoe. There was no fixed contract and the owners would pay as and when their horse was shod. Bob was probably about thirty and near enough square; he may well have had gypsy connections, certainly he came from a large Cockney tribe. He also owned a couple of saluki lurchers which were his pride and joy and I suspect made him some money at illegal coursing. Susan got on well with him; he used to complain to her, "Sue I can't get motivated; some of these punters, if I put the shoes on the wrong way round, they wouldn't notice."

One day, she decided to sack him. It caused total consternation in the yard. "Had she found another farrier?" "It hadn't been easy but yes, she had." This was even worse; the prospect of a second farrier in the yard worried everyone. People spoke in hushed voices. In the middle of all this the two protagonists stayed calm; Bob said, "You don't need to worry about us, Sue, we big guys don't fight, we'd do each other far too much harm."

Before he ever arrived, the new farrier managed to fall off his motor bike, so he never did appear in the yard and Bob carried on as usual.

Bob had a property in Surrey. It was part of a large estate which had been sold in two parts and must have been at least fifty acres. I asked him once how he managed to afford it; "My friend XXXX (the owner) owed me." As an answer it left a lot of questions hanging in the air. We used to take our horses there for their summer holiday and met his wife and two boys. We called the boys the clones. Bob was extremely proud of them, "I don't want them to be like their Dad, all muscle and no brain." He himself was illiterate; on the other hand he did know the Latin names for all the parts of the horse's hoof – it was part of the farrier's exams.

There was a problem with Bob's estate. The M25 ran right through the middle of it. Fortunately, the motorway was quite high above field level, which reduced the noise and gave room for a tunnel underneath it. What it did do was provide access to all the villains in London who could park on the hard-shoulder and get straight down to Bob's fields.

A year or two before, Bob had been grazing some polo ponies; they were valuable animals – they came complete with their own groom. One morning, the groom came down, noticed they were standing oddly, hanging their heads. When she rushed to look at them they had all been attacked with a hammer, a blow to the top of each one's head. Amazingly quite a lot of them survived.

Presumably someone owed someone and hadn't paid.

Weekends we used to ride across to Wimbledon Common. This involved crossing the A3 at the Robin Hood roundabout; to cross the A3 (there were traffic lights) we had a short lead between the two dogs, connected in turn to a 'leading rein' about five foot long which we could hold while riding. It looked a bit alarming but worked perfectly, mainly for the reason that all the animals were enjoying themselves. The only time I had a problem was once crossing back into Richmond Park on a part of the roundabout where the traffic was moving very slowly, a driver came straight towards me, looking sideways at the houses with no sign of being aware I was straight in front of him. Fortunately the driver behind him realised what was happening and hooted loudly and he woke up. I've always been grateful to that man.

When I got nearer to retiring age, I started riding before going to work, when the park opened at dawn. This was straightforward enough in summer, but presented problems in winter when it opened so late it restricted my riding time. I used to go over just before seven – I had a key to the yard – collect the horse and our two dogs and used to join the queue of taxi drivers waiting to go and play golf. My top party trick was to open the yard doors, they were big six foot wooden doors, from the back of the horse while leading the dogs, turn the horse and dogs and shut the doors after us – perfect harmony between man and beasts. Not that anyone noticed.

I never tired of Richmond Park, and some of those early morning rides were magical. Especially in autumn, when it was often misty and the stags would be rutting, there was strange mooing and bellowing followed by the rattle of antlers – it seemed a world away from suburban Surrey outside. One morning – it must have been spring as the sun was very low – I saw the mist in a cloud over Pen Ponds with the sun shining through it looking exactly like a scene painted by Turner.

I used to get about an hour's ride. Then it was only a matter of putting the dogs on the lead to negotiate the traffic coming out of the Park, getting back to the stables, stabling the horse and a quick (fairly) dash through the park and on the train to Waterloo.

One morning about seven o'clock, when it was still pitch dark, looking for somewhere to park the car near the stables, I was flagged down by a man and a girl. The man looked pretty agitated, "I found this lady wandering all over the place." She certainly wasn't dressed for it, having on a nightie and manifestly nothing else. He said, "She must have come from the Priory," (a nursing home and rehabilitation centre just up the road), "could you take her there?" So she got into the passenger seat and he promptly vanished. I should mention she was about twenty and extremely pretty; and heavily sedated.

I visualised two scenarios, one that she would try to climb out of the car and get killed or injured, or two that she would stay in the car and accuse me of assault; or any permutation of the two. I also visualised a few headlines, all beginning " Lloyd's Underwriter" – Lloyd's was getting a sufficiently bad press at the time that the public would happily have believed that abduction and rape could be now added to the list of our offences.

As it turned out I needn't have worried. The sedatives came to my rescue – she must have been on some veterinary scale of dosage – and she sat quietly in the car while I drove to the Priory and went to find, and excoriate, the duty orderly. The Priory seemed to take it in their stride.

I kept a horse box in the stable yard. I could never quite make out why it was tolerated as it was terribly in the way. I think the Whites must have felt it gave the yard a certain touch of class. Beauty was definitely in the eye of the beholder as like a lot of its type it was a specialised body fixed on an incredibly ancient Bedford TK 7.5 ton truck. As it would hold four horses it contributed to the social life of the yard, enabling me to take friends to shows and events which otherwise would not have been possible for them.

Sponsored rides had been developed all round south west London and were good fun. Normally they involved a ten or fifteen mile ride with as many as thirty jumps which were optional, over country that one normally didn't get a chance to see. Susan and I went regularly on them and they made for very social riding.

They must have taken a lot of work to organise but brought in big money, as much as twenty thousand pounds on the day. Susan didn't jump very much but I loved it. My favourite was at RAF Halton near Aylesbury; there were some good composite cross country jumps and it finished with a sort of steeple-chase round the airfield. The final jump, which all the spectators congregated around to watch, was an aircraft fuselage. It was big but inviting, and because the fuselage was long – wide as one rode towards it, it didn't look so high and the horses just flew it.

Another form of riding which I really enjoyed was team-chasing. Proper team-chasing is extremely professional and highly competitive, but Ian Balding, the race horse trainer, hosted a meet on his gallops which included one race called 'Fun and Easy' which was just our ticket. The idea is that you have a team of four, timed over a course, and the fastest team wins. You can usually discard the slowest rider's score. The jumps are normal cross-country jumps, though sometimes there is a sheep pen into which the whole team must have jumped before anyone can jump out again. Because they think they are racing each other, the horses all go much faster and jump more willingly than usual, so if you can control them, it's most exhilarating.

Me, team chasing with Quest

I used to get a team together from the yard and a friend who was Chairman of Charlton Football Club provided four of their strips which made us look uniform if not respectable. They were surprisingly shiny. One year we got over-excited enough to go in for an open team-chase near Farringdon. I managed to assemble a slightly classier team than usual. We got there late and rushed to walk the course. Halfway round we came to a ditch which looked ten foot wide and six foot deep; it wasn't of course, but it was big enough for me to be sure I wouldn't get my horse over it; so I didn't bother with walking the rest of it. Come our turn, I latched on to one of our team who had done some serious hunting. Her horse sailed over the ditch, so mine did too and I spent the rest of the course wondering where on earth to go. We did get round.

CHAPTER 17

Our time at Roehampton Stables ceased abruptly and oddly. In the cause of rescuing a woman doctor from Kingston Hospital, who had been out on one of their group rides and whose on-call bleeper had got locked in the office, Susan rang Nick White's home number. She spoke to his wife – a perfectly sensible conversation. Ten minutes later, Nick was on the phone, seemingly incandescent with rage at someone ringing his home number, demanding that our horses and the lorry be out of the yard by the following day. I do remember thinking a new definition of loneliness might be having suddenly to find a park for a 7.5 ton truck in the London suburbs.

By that time we fortunately weren't tied to Richmond Park, had even become slightly bored with it, so we moved our team down to Byfleet, half an hour down the A3. Riding stables are not often boring places but we never quite replicated the fun we had at Roehampton.

All the time we were fooling around with horses, we also sometimes moved around by car.

Some people bring with them into adult life the memory of some traumatic event in childhood, causing them greater or lesser misery as they age. My memory was hardly serious but it still persisted. It was of my parents' car. It was called a Ford Popular. This was an early example of nomenclature which invited retribution, in much the same class as the Austin Allegro, which was quickly converted by unkind critics into 'Allegro ma non troppo.'

As far I was concerned the Popular definitely wasn't, and when Susan and I finally came to part with the Lambretta – we did this quite literally when a tyre burst going round a roundabout in rush hour traffic – we tried to find something a bit more interesting than the Popular, although at least as cheap.

An acquaintance of mine in Lloyd's had the reputation of knowing of cars for sale and for fifty pounds he produced a 1935 Triumph Gloria. The name wasn't perfect but we couldn't afford to be hidebound. It had a fairly sporty image, boasted a Coventry Climax engine and would cruise at about fifty miles an hour. Even in those days not very fast. For added excitement it was fitted with a free-wheel device.You unscrewed a thing looking like a stop-cock next to the hand brake and now the engine freewheeled. This was intended to save fuel - not a very important consideration then - at the expense of any ability to brake using the engine and generally playing havoc with the handling of the car. The only time I used it, I narrowly avoided going into the back of a police car. In any case the brakes weren't terribly good - none of them were in those days.

In the course of its twenty five years, the clutch had started to malfunction. The remedy for this was to open the clutch housing (fairly easily accessible) and tip carbon tetrachloride into the clutch while carefully slipping it. This would clean the oil off the clutch which was causing the problem. As a technique, this has fallen foul of fears about the carcinogenic properties of carbon-tet, which I believe is no longer readily available. It was in any case a bit messy for your average daily commute. We got to Cornwall and back in the Triumph, but decided to move on.

Next on the list was a Mark 1 Landrover which belonged to an Australian friend of my father. He was retired and, being extremely Anglophile, had worked out a lifestyle based on living in a cottage in Herefordshire (with no road access whatever) and towing his caravan round Europe in winter. Susan and I had visited Jay and his wife, which involved sleeping in the caravan. It was very stuffy and opening the window resulted in my waking in the morning from a nightmare which turned out to be due to a cow licking my forehead.

Unfortunately, the tax man had woken up to the fact that Jay was paying little or no tax and he had had to leave abruptly, giving rise to the need to sell us the Landrover. It wasn't a great success; it didn't go any faster than the Triumph and made much more noise. We had planned to make a trip to Yugoslavia which involved going by train from Dusseldorf to southern Austria; unfortunately the Landrover had a metal cover enclosing the back which was too high to fit on the train. So I made a canvas cover to fit instead. It was hard work and collateral damage was the destruction of Susan's sewing machine. Although it would have kept the rain out if it had rained, it didn't work very well as the opening at the rear drew in dust and on the un-mettalled roads of Yugoslavia we would arrive at our destination looking like 'scene of crime officers' or mortuary attendants. In addition the starter motor gave up and we discovered the delights of the starting handle.

We were once more ready for a change, so back to my chum in Lloyd's. His next production, also for fifty pounds, was called a Humber Super Snipe, although why anyone should want to associate such an elegant and agile bird with a car built like a tank and with the manoeuvrability of a hippo, was not apparent. This one was four years old, had done about twenty thousand miles and was in good condition.

New, it had sold for about £1100. Rolls Royce had an advertisement, "The only sound you hear is the clock on the dashboard ticking." The Humber was quiet but in our case the sound you heard was the slurp of petrol going through the carburettor. The engine was four and a quarter litres and, on the school run, it managed about eight miles to the gallon. On one weekend trip to see our friends the Coopers in north Wales, we got through forty five gallons of petrol.

The other expenditure was on tyres. With huge weight and sloppy suspension it got through tyres prodigiously. For long trips it was advisable to adjust the tick-over speed to nearly nothing to get the benefit of the enormous engine to assist braking. As with all our cars at the time, braking was not its best feature. We kept it for about five years and when we eventually came to take it to the breakers yard (it cost a fee of 2/6) I found someone had overnight jacked it up and removed a front wheel; I would willingly have let them have the whole car and given them 2/6. Susan rather enjoyed driving it; the steering column gear change was hopelessly sloppy (this suited her style) and the engine was so powerful it hardly mattered if you were in the wrong gear. I used to get reports of it being driven round Kingston apparently unmanned, but that was simply because she didn't come above the steering wheel.

Next on the list was the AC Saloon – no nonsense about fancy names – it was a saloon car made by the AC car company of Thames Ditton. This was the favourite car of all the family, who on the whole tended to be sick in cars and didn't much like them. It was comfortable, not too noisy, and extremely elegant in appearance and it went quicker than most of our previous cars. It also had more wrong with it than any car we ever owned.

It was after we had taken it on a family holiday in northern Spain, an adventure trip over the Picos de Europa that our troubles began. The only symptom was that the rear number plate had started to lift. The bodywork was aluminium on a wooden frame and some rummaging about in the boot and the removal of a lot of rotten woodwork, revealed that the main chassis member, a steel girder shaped as a C had now corroded to become a single flexible flat strip of metal – hence the lifting number plate.

The first thing to do was to get it an MOT certificate; slightly to my surprise this wasn't a problem, (I may have inadvertantly left the boot locked) so now I could drive it to the workshop of a couple of BEAC welders, moonlighting as Rogers and Hart, who took time off from rebuilding Boeing 737's to reconstruct our rear end. There was a thriving AC Cars Club, engaged in racing the saloons as well as the AC sports cars, so their services were frequently needed. In this case I'm not sure they got the geometry quite right as afterwards the car would skid alarmingly off a cats-eye or some unevenness in the road.

This wasn't the end of our problems as one day when we were cruising down the M4 there was a loud bang and I saw the distributor lying in the road. There was also a hole in the side of the crankcase. Getting a new engine involved being towed by a friend from Maidenhead to Bromley. He did have a history of alcoholism, though as far as I could judge he was reasonably sober this time, and beggars can't be choosers. It did seem an awfully long way.

By the time I had bought a new engine and twice removed and ground down the cylinder head, I began to feel I had had enough and passed it on to another optimist.

After the AC I gradually moved into the world of proper (and more boring cars) although there were still exciting moments, for example when I took Susan to a British Leyland dealer and at one point one of the salesmen told her that "Madam would lose her charisma in a Marina" - maybe I shouldn't have laughed but that young man was never going to make a sale. I felt some sympathy with him - try saying it quickly and without practice.

Around this time we owned a Triumph 2500 saloon. This was a nice car; it went well, cornered properly, looked pleasant. It had two unusual features. One was overdrive (a kind of substitute for a fourth forward gear) which was operated electrically by a switch on the top of the gear lever. I never did discover whether it actually did anything; it was possible that the switch wasn't even connected.

The other more significant feature was not strictly to do with design. It happened that at that time, Surrey Police had a fleet of Triumph 2500, all plain white and looking exactly like ours. This had the effect that whenever we hove in sight, all the traffic in front reverted to just below legal speed limits. While fun in its way, it could be rather irritating, especially as even when overtaking was possible, there was still the chance of a genuine police car lurking among the traffic.

After the British Leyland episode, Susan took no part in buying cars but reserved the right to criticise my choice, notably an excursion into boy-racer country with an Alfa-Romeo fitted with a turbo-charger and a sunshine roof that leaked badly. After that it was middle age and sensible company cars like a BMW 325; although it did have a 'close ratio' gearbox and sports suspension which I didn't mention to Susan - she was never very interested in the technical side of things - and it served me well for over twenty years.

CHAPTER 18

Kids and Coopers 1963/70

When we moved to Queens Road at the end of 1963, our neighbours on the Park side, the Macnairs, were already there and our neighbours on the other side, the Gimlettes, moved in shortly afterwards. I look back with gratitude on being blessed with such good neighbours; perhaps other people are just as lucky, but we have remained friends for fifty years.

The neighbourhood may have contributed. Studying the title deeds of 22 Queens Road, when we came to leave after thirty years, I found we had been only the sixth family to live there in the hundred and twenty eight years since it was built. Possibly more important, was that all the houses, which were arranged in a large triangle, perhaps eight or ten houses to each of the three streets making up the triangle, were broadly similar in size and style; they were ideal for young families and I suspect that, just as ours had changed hands regularly but infrequently, the others had kept roughly in step, so that a large proportion of our neighbours were at exactly the same stage of family life – right at the beginning.

The houses were mostly detached but quite close together so a certain amount of give and take had to be exercised. Early on I learnt that our neighbour Ruth was uneasy because our bedroom window looked straight into her bathroom. I felt the neighbourly thing to do was to make her a modesty garment, a simple classic design to place over the bath, made of opaque plastic sheeting with a hole for the head and weights at intervals round the edge so that it could be draped round the bath without falling into it; nicely wrapped for Christmas, it made an acceptable present.

In fact our window was five feet up, with a chest of drawers in front of it, so Susan might well have become uneasy if I had spent the evening standing on the chest of drawers with a pair of binoculars. However, as always, it's the gesture which counts; perhaps it contributed to our remaining friends for the next fifty or so years.

One summer, six or seven of us got the habit of playing tennis every Saturday on the local courts. Part of the fun was going down to the courts in Archie Macnair's new Roller. Anyone sitting out a session could loll in comfort in the Rolls. One day, Susan was doing this and having a strong element of Pandora in her, started playing with knobs and switches. After a bit we heard the horn sound, attention was drawn and it turned out Susan had completely locked the Roller from the inside and also that Archie had left his keys in the car for safety. It's difficult to get into an expensive car if you haven't got a key and don't know how it came to be locked. Oh, and you can't communicate with the lady inside except by signals.

Another thing which contributed to getting to know families in the area was the Queens Road Dames School. Colin and Mary Prince have been part of our life for so long now that I can't remember how we met. We rapidly came to see a very great deal of Mary when she and Susan decided to open a pre-primary school together.

Mary is a qualified teacher whereas Susan was a lab assistant trained in haematology, which was less obviously useful, but on the other hand our house was just about big enough, and with a reasonable garden, to run the school there. My function was to look after the accounts and act as general carpenter and dogsbody, to make and maintain Wendy Houses and the like.

One of the problems with running a school like that was the shortness of the age span it catered for. It was definitely not a child minding crèche, so in practise three was about the youngest we would accept and they were off to primary school at five so it was a rapid turnover. On top of this, the parents only paid for time the children were actually in the school, so there was apt to be some absenteeism. We were licensed for twenty children but in practise had a few more than that on the books to allow for absentees. Once or twice, when the inspector came round, it was necessary to keep the kids moving as fast as possible to avoid over-accurate counting. We never had any trouble and I think it was regarded as well run.

What was surprising was the number of parents who became our friends through it, and the number of adults who now remind me they were at the school. I suppose it must have lasted about five or six years, long enough for our friends' children to pass through and for it to become much less fun when all the parents were total strangers.

Emma was born on the 17th March 1964. Unlike the arrival of her brother and sister it was no more stressful than normal.

Catherine had been born in the Hammersmith Hospital. When the moment came, we headed for the hospital and were directed round to a small side door of the maternity wing, it opened briefly, Susan was snatched inside and the door was slammed in my face. Thirty six hours later I was allowed back; as it happened there had been a cloud burst by then and the ward was a foot deep in water. Husbands were definitely regarded as surplus to requirements.

Charlie was very nearly born on the Cromwell Road Extension; we paused there on our way home from a totally unnecessary drive round St John's Wood which Susan had demanded, and managed to telephone our GP who arrived at Chancellor's Street at the same moment as we did. She at once took charge and decided that the dog (our miniature poodle) could stay, to avoid jealousy. It was not an easy birth and the midwife's arrival coincided with the poodles coming out from under the bed and being sick, which upset the midwife dreadfully. She made an awful fuss, which considering she had contributed precisely nothing to the proceedings was unacceptable.

This wasn't the end of a difficult day. Susan was downstairs with the baby and I slept in our bedroom on the ground floor. I was woken by cries from down below and I remembered that the thermostat on our (brand new) hot water cylinder had gone wrong and I had switched to over-ride, fine as long as one remembered to switch it off; which I hadn't. So now we had hot water coming out of the cold taps and steam coming out of the hot and in general an intimation that the whole thing was going to explode. It upset the dog too.

From the time of Emma's birth, it was definitely family holidays – there were five of us. We decided on going to Wales and I was deputed to find a farm that would have us. In those days, telephoning somewhere in Wales involved getting through to a main Welsh exchange and asking for the number – not easy when you couldn't pronounce the exchange you wanted and couldn't understand the lady at the main exchange.

Eventually I got through to a Mrs Davies, near St David's, pretty much as far west as one could go. She was deeply suspicious; she never advertised, how had I got her number? When I mentioned that we were prepared to come in June, outside school holidays, she relented a lot and we signed up to a deal. It was a mixed farm, just her and her husband; her son was away at college.

Our journey started early and it took forever, the Severn crossing was not even half way. When we got there, the farm building was an ordinary small farmhouse, the same as you see all around the West Country. We had no idea it would turn out to be magic.

On the other hand, there was nothing ordinary about Mrs Davies; on the stout side and overwhelmingly jolly – not Welsh she told us, as she came from Haverfordwest (the market town about six miles up the road) -but you couldn't tell; it was a sort of local joke. Her husband was tall and quiet and kindly.

Farming in England, certainly in the home counties, had by now started to be industrialised. This seemed like a scene from a century before. I think they may have had a tractor, though most equipment was borrowed on a sharing arrangement from one of the neighbouring small farms. The description 'mixed' hardly did it justice; there were cattle, pigs, a farm horse, ducks, chicken and geese, all mingling round the yard and the duck pond. There was a hedged enclosure where Mrs Davies hung her washing; every now and then there would be an emergency when the heifers got in with it.

They had had a sow which had learnt how to get into the feed-store – on the kitchen wall was one of those aerial photographs of the farm which one gets inveigled into buying; this one showed the sow manipulating the latch with her snout.

While the hedgerows in Surrey were completely sterile, in West Pembrokeshire they were full of wildflowers and I distinctly remember a mass of yellowhammers, as common there as hedge sparrows.

There was a proper stream which ran right outside the front door of the cottage and the farm house was definitely damp, the wallpaper bubbled badly. By the time she was two, this was too much of a temptation for Em and she stripped the lot. Mrs Davies just roared with laughter. A toad managed to find its way under the front door. Mrs Davies had a fit of hysterics so Charlie, aged about three, who was fond of toads, removed it for her, earning endless gratitude. Em was about three months old when we first went; Mr Davies insisted that she should have her milk straight from the cow, having wiped the udder down with what appeared to be a floor cloth. We concentrated on the likely benefit to her immune system and hoped for the best.

The loo was outside, round the side of the house. In the night, one had to negotiate one's way past the dogs, three border collies, who camped round the back door. They were friendly and looked out for a bit of chat on the way. It wasn't good when it rained. Sunday in West Wales was particularly testing; it was extremely difficult to get food and drink was definitely off.

Some people might have thought these were serious disadvantages, but they didn't count. It really *was* magic.

The beaches were hard to get to, but were well worth the effort. Of course it was sunny most of the time and it never rained – I have pictures to prove it. We went there for three years consecutively until time caught up with us; we could no longer ignore school terms and Mrs Davies' other regular clients were only parted from her by death, so we had to give up.

Our three children, Charlie, Catherine and Emma 1966

About six or seven years ago, we made a pilgrimage to West Pembrokeshire. It was as though a malign magician had erased all the best bits. To be honest, the absence of wild flowers and song birds was probably more to do with the fact that it was Christmas than to any evil enchantment, but we never found the farm. Perhaps it was just as well. By now it would have been absorbed into a much larger and more efficient unit and the house would have been someone's second home.

It was very easy for us to idealise the Davies' life but it must have been tough. I discovered that the space needed to let the house for families like ours, was only achieved by the Davies themselves spending the summer living in an old railway goods wagon parked in the orchard. In winter, the damp must have been horrendous and although Mr Davies had security of tenure on the farm, it was doubtful whether his son would be able to take over the farm and more particularly the house. This was a difficult question and one to which the Davies' certainly didn't know the answer.

Back in Surrey, I used to commute daily from Norbiton station to Waterloo. There were the last remnants of steam locomotion still around. The commuter trains were all electric of course, but we had a small goods yard at Norbiton with a coal-fired shunting engine. It didn't do very much but emitted clouds of black smoke, which, when the wind was in the east, engulfed us.

We smile at the pictures of city men wearing their regulation bowlers, but hats were needed to keep one's hair half-way clean. Today it's difficult to visualise quite how dirty London was, with coal-fired steam engines and literally thousands, perhaps hundreds of thousands, of coal fires heating not just the terrace houses but even, as my mother discovered, the 'Ear Nose and Throat' ward of a London teaching hospital.

My first winter in the city was before the 'Clean Air Act' came into force and it was better than the preceding one, when there had been considerable loss of life, but was still quite bad. One day, the fog got into Lloyd's and we could no longer see from one side of the underwriting room to the other. Outside, it was like one of Conan Doyle's descriptions of a 'pea souper.' Then the 'Clean Air Act' came in and it all ceased. It was remarkable.

Our friends the Coopers had bought a house in Islington a year or two after we moved into Queens Road. As sometimes happened to them, the house needed a major rebuild and the first winter was spent with Accrow props where the back wall should have been. Pat, of course, totally disregarded the problems this caused with cooking but bathing was a major difficulty, so they all used to come over to us for a bath at the weekend.

These were great social occasions and Pat used to help things along by calling in at Smithfield on the way. 11 o'clock on a Saturday morning was prime time for a bargain at Smithfield. There was one particular joint of lamb which had clearly gone a step too far in its hanging. Pat and I took it down to the cellar away from everyone else and set to work on it, wiping it with cloths dipped in vinegar. It did smell and there were even a couple of maggots, but we cleaned it up and it disappeared straight into the oven. It was delicious and made me realise that the Victorian partiality for meat served 'high', particularly game, depended largely on the people who ate it not having anything to do with its preparation.

When we first moved to Kingston we were extremely interested in anything which would bring in some cash. Emma's arrival in the world meant that for a time the two servants' rooms at the back of the house were occupied but once these became free, we were able to have a lodger – the choir master at Tiffins School in Kingston. After a while he moved to another school and his successor Bruce Pullan came into our lives and, though he has lived in North America for nearly the last fifty years, has stayed in our lives ever since.

Bruce had a degree from Cambridge where he had been a King's Choral Scholar and had also acquired a taste for good living which he shared with us and undid some of the benefits of the rent he paid. He certainly made up for this in entertainment value.

Susan had put on her schoolmistress' hat when formulating rules for the behaviour of lodgers. These were effective with Bruce for about the first five minutes. After that he became part of the family. Apart from brightening our lives with occasional gourmet meals, he would give impromptu music lessons to the kids. He murmured once that he had never thought when he started at Kings College that he would finish up trying to teach someone, who was completely tone deaf, how to play the viola.

Bruce was married from our house. There was a slight complication in that he and his fiancee had actually been living somewhere else and Bruce had failed to mention this to his parents. Meanwhile, I had filled his room with bits of central heating gear, so it was better if his parents didn't go upstairs and see it. In addition to this, we had still got our ageing poodle, first acquired at the time we were married. This had developed diabetes which Susan was treating with injections of insulin, but on the morning of the wedding it suddenly became very ill, haemorrhaging everywhere, and had to be put down. So the day was not free from problems.

There was a difficult time just before Bruce and Lynn finally moved to Canada. They had sold their house at the beginning of one of the London property booms and then found there was literally nothing which they could afford to buy as, overnight, prices had rocketed. So they stayed with one lot of friends and fed with us, which would have worked better if we hadn't been in the middle of taking the dining room chimney out and so had to go outside to get from one end of the house to the other.

As to teaching tone-deaf violists, Bruce needn't have worried; after immigrating to Canada in 1974 he became extremely successful as a choirmaster, conductor, soloist singer and an eminent figure on the West Coast of North America, finally decorated by the Canadian government with the Canada Medal. We had several later visits; he normally travelled accompanied by thirty or so choristers all set to entertain the locals.

CHAPTER 19

Settling in, in Surrey 1963/84

We lived at No 22 Queens Road for exactly thirty years; we seem always to have moved house on the twenty first of September - for no considered reason - though I did believe it to be the Feast of St Maurice, I was actually out in my calculations by one day. My memory of when particular things happened is totally imprecise, so the 'middle' of our time there was 1973 to 1983 and the ten years before and after were the 'beginning' and the 'end.'

The story of how Susan became one of the very first people to be breathalysed belongs to the beginning. It happened that on the day the law came into force (at 6pm on the dot), we had arranged to meet some friends at a pub in Chelsea and then go out to dinner. We were a little early, time enough for me to have a pint. When our friends turned up, we went to get into our car, parked just outside the pub; Susan pointed out that she'd had only a soft drink and moreover, had better experience of driving our Humber with its completely erratic gear change.

Anyway we swapped over, getting a loud cheer from the crowd outside the pub and as we drove away, a police car duly pulled out to follow. After a polite interval we were stopped and Susan was breathalysed. No result of course. But we were behind schedule. We explained to the Irish woman running the restaurant and at the same time noticed three Cabinet Ministers -Crossman, Packenham and a third – at a table together. She proceeded to give them absolute stick about passing a law that harassed her clients as well as making them late for dinner, very loudly so that everyone in the restaurant heard. Not necessarily the best way to run a restaurant, but good entertainment.

During the middle period, our friends the Coopers were living in a village in France called Mont Saxonnez. It was an idyllic spot half way up the mountain but the Coopers had put their own gloss on it – 'The Sound of Music' meets 'Steptoe and Son.'

This was mainly due to Dan's policy about cars; he liked to have several at any given time, distributed round various key points in Europe. In addition there was a specific problem at this period. As I touched on earlier, Dan worked for the United Nations in Geneva as did a lot of his friends. The American and Canadian staff tended to bring over their own cars and sell them when they left. This upset the Swiss and French customs as the cars had come in under diplomatic plates or something similar and were definitely not supposed to be sold on, even within the United Nations.

Sometimes there was a gap in the way the regulations applied; thus the Coopers had an enormous Dodge which was legal in France but not in Switzerland and there was a Studebaker that was definitely 'hot' in both countries and had frequently to be moved around, preferably at night. There was a residue from all this car dealing which finished up in the Cooper's garden and contributed to the Steptoe image.

Inevitably there were major building works going on; one side of the house gave literal expression to the term 'curtain wall' as it consisted of plastic sheeting through which a feral cat used to attack the labour force, a somewhat unpleasant individual, a 'brickie', whom Dan had signed up at the Islington labour exchange, who used to sleep just inside the plastic.

The parts of the house which were finished were absolutely stunning, though there were eccentricities. Pat had brought from New York an extremely large fridge/freezer, which of course was designed to run at 110 volts; so a transformer was necessary which was connected by a two pin plug, as is the way of things in France. So if you disconnected the plug, to clean or defrost the freezer say, you had exactly a fifty/fifty chance of re-connecting it with the chassis, door handle etc. live. Fortunately at 110 rather than 240 volts.

No one had actually worked this out and the approved remedy was to hang a towel on the door handle and use that for opening it. Curiously, even after I got home I found I had an innate reluctance to open a fridge without using a towel on the handle.

Dan worked as a translator at the United Nations, in the 'Summary Record' rather than 'Simultaneous' department. This meant that at the end of the day he had to translate the speeches into English and at the same time write a precis. Bearing in mind that the majority of the speeches were made by delegates anxious to prove to the 'folks back home' (i.e. their employers) that they were doing something to earn their exorbitant salaries, the speeches tended to be long on words, but short in content, the only requirement being to get them into the summary record for home publication.

This didn't make for stimulating work translating them. Dan introduced me to some of his colleagues; they were all highly intelligent and bored out of their minds by what they were paid to do.

Dan got to know the typists very well; he worked on the principle that he was only required to get to work early enough, to allow sufficient time for the typists to work on the draft so that they could present it at midday for review. Dan had worked this out as being eleven o'clock, but there was apt to be slippage. Moreover no one else shared his view.

There was a further problem about his employment. While he was in England Dan had spotted a commercial opportunity. People owning caravans, permanently parked in caravan parks, tended to have contracts which allowed the landlords to force them to sell off their caravans, when they were still relatively new, in order to maintain the 'quality' of the caravans in the Park. Needless to say they didn't get much for them and at least in Dan's eyes, the caravans had plenty of years life in them. Why not buy up some of these and use them for holiday lets in France?

All that was needed was a low-loader and a basic work-force – both readily available round Islington and parts East. Dan managed to get all this under way, found some sites for the caravans not too far from the south coast and began happily running the business from his office in the United Nations.

Unfortunately quite a lot of people were out to put a stop to it. The French authorities claimed that the caravans had never been through customs; this was inescapable but Dan claimed that they had actually refused to register them. There was a prosecution in which the judge was shown a photograph of one of the sites and said how delightful it looked, which wasn't what the prosecution, who had produced the photograph, wanted to hear. But at the end of it all, they confiscated the caravans (fortunately they really were very cheap) and Dan was booted out of the United Nations. Probably he had simply managed to upset too many people. He had had a good run there, possibly six or seven years and he and Pat still had the house at Mont Saxonnez.

Eventually Dan and Pat returned to England and started living in a flat in Putney. As always with Dan, this was not straightforward. The flat belonged to his brother Paul with whom relations were extremely bad. The background to how this situation came about was complicated. For reasons never fully explained, Paul at some point had needed the flat not to be in his name, so he had made it over to Dan's son Sean, who had now let his parents live in it. We became involved because during part of this time Sean was living with us; and Paul wanted the flat back.

My own relations with Paul, in so far as they existed at all, were poor. For some reason which I can't now remember he had come to dinner with us and half way through, I had ordered him out saying, "You are not welcome here." It sounds quite pompous, and goodness knows what it was about but it seems as though relations were poor.

Some of the endless negotiations must have taken place before Sean had come to live with us because I have three letters, one from Sean, one from Dan and one from Tuthill (Dan's father) all trying to involve me in what looked like becoming a court case.

Dan's letter is seriously threatening on the basis that if I side with Paul, even by omission, he will treat it as a hostile act; Tuthill's, written on Paul's behalf, is far more emollient and includes the suggestion that I talk it over informally with his friend Platts-Mills, at that time an extremely eminent QC. Sean's is rather confused.

The concealed threat in Dan's letter was that he had a real taste for litigating in person. The courts, with what seemed a completely ludicrous sense of fair play assumed that a 'litigant in person' was the underdog in need of assistance, which in Dan's case was the reverse of the truth. Round about this time, the Office of Fair Trading or some such body had brought a case against him in relation to his caravan holiday business. Spurning the offer of bail he had elected to be held in Wandsworth gaol and retired to the prison library to prepare a case which ultimately broke records both for length, lack of purpose and complexity at (I think) Southwark Crown Court.

Declining Tuthill's offer to let Platts-Mills make mincemeat of me but without letting myself get sucked in by Dan, I somehow managed to avoid getting involved. Somewhere about this time I remember Susan getting a letter from Dan which caused her alarm enough to say, "Do you think he is going to sue me?" I was mean enough to tease her with the suggestion that, if he did, there wasn't enough money in the world to employ a barrister and she would have to fight the case herself. It was one of the very few occasions when I saw her seriously rattled.

Dan had a small fleet of Fiat 500 'Topolinos', none of them in show-room condition; these were his standard method of transport, so when he decided to make a trip to Oxford, one of these came into play. The occasion was a visit to a cousin, who happened to be Principal of Somerville College with a view to helping get Cathy, his elder daughter, into Oxford. I don't think much came of the visit but the journey was memorable. The Fiat was in 'three seater configuration' – that is to say, the front passenger seat was missing, so Pat and Cathy had to sit at the back. Problems arose somewhere out in the country, when the car got a flat tyre. Fortunately this happened directly outside a police station, so Dan was able to display his negotiating skills in persuading a young policeman to help him change one bald tyre for another and thankfully send them on their way – this, without road tax or insurance even being mentioned. I think the local police probably just wanted Dan off their patch as quickly as possible.

Dan was very large, very bright and a very loyal friend (which didn't preclude occasional threats of legal action which were more or less his life blood). He believed family life involved conflict. There was a family cottage in North Wales, halfway up a mountain. We went there twice; the first time he had an argument with Matthew, his youngest son, whom he banished upstairs for the evening. Matthew retaliated by dropping nails on his father's bald head through knot holes in the floorboards; then as it grew darker (there was no electricity) slipping quietly down to join the party. Everyone but Dan knew – or maybe he did too.

The second trip to the cottage was for his younger daughter Louise's christening, aged seven. Susan was godmother. My function was to clear the chapel, reputedly the oldest in Wales, of sand. It was on the beach and there was at least a ton of sand inside to shift. There was a good party including Doug,

Dan's partner from Rentavilla days. At the end of the party, Dan didn't want Doug to leave, so he stole his ignition keys. Doug eventually got them back and in retaliation went off with Dan's shoes, size 13, and not easily replaceable in North Wales. Dan was last seen mournfully walking barefoot round Barmouth.

Some time during our last ten years at Queens Road, Dan suddenly died. He had been living with Pat in a cottage in a remote part of Spain when one day he suddenly dropped a suitcase; it was the very first indication of a brain tumour. His lifelong eccentricity had nothing to do with his final illness – I believe the surgeon at the Marsden became quite fretful explaining to his numerous friends that the cancer, an extremely aggressive one, really had started only a few months before his death.

Around this time Sean, Dan's eldest son spent about three years living with us. Most of that time he was working in a bar and used to come home late; in 1980 he was joined for a spell in the summer vacation by his sister Cathy and her boyfriend Colin, down from university. Our three were all still at home, so the house was busy. One lunchtime Sean said, "You know you've got a poltergeist?' We didn't, but now we came to think of it, there had been times when Susan was alone in the house and had heard strange noises from the room above the kitchen. Nothing was ever damaged so, as poltergeists go, this one was quite domesticated, its manifestations, according to Sean, being limited to crashing and banging around in the kitchen. It is suggested that they are associated with teenagers and we certainly met that criterion.

It was not unknown for some of Sean's friends to use drugs. Our Springer spaniel 'Wellie' who spent quite a lot of time with Sean, previously used to turn right out of the house towards the Park, now tended to turn left – towards the pub. On one occasion he was reported to have eaten £30 worth of cannabis, seemingly without modifying his usual rather regrettable behaviour, but considerably diminishing his popularity with Sean's friends.

Then there was the affair of the cannabis plant. This was Sean's contribution to the general decor. Its arrival happened to coincide with a visit from the police – more social than police business and concluding with a drink on the terrace. Quite soon I realised that the plant was on full display on a window ledge just above the policeman's head. When it was time for him to leave, it was most important that he didn't turn round, so we all gathered round and ushered him out. I wonder what he thought? Or did he know? The visit from Nico slotted into this quite well…

It must have been 1979 or 1980 when Sean had been abroad; on his return he would normally have let himself in with his key, but this time he rang the doorbell. I found him on the doorstep with a woman, apparently aged about sixty, and a large wooden box. He said, "This is Nico." With the air of someone who had removed any doubt there might have been. I had never really managed to keep track of Sean's social life, but I was pretty sure a Nico didn't feature; so who was she? Rather wildly, I thought about salads but that clearly wasn't the answer. Then there was the wooden box. There is supposed to be a link between function and form but this didn't help much – it looked just like a wooden box.

It was perhaps unfortunate that at the time I was one of the few people in England who hadn't heard of Nico. Nico, whoever she was, was clearly in a bad way; cold turkey came to mind. It was also clear that she was having a lot of trouble getting around, in fact Sean had rescued her on the cross channel ferry, and knowing a great deal more than I did about the pop music scene, immediately identified the wooden box as the harmonium which was her signature instrument.

He must also have come in handy for carrying it. I never heard the full details of the journey from Dover to Kingston but it must have been fairly epic.

I suppose it must have been fortunate for Nico to find people willing to look after her, even if a family Sunday lunch wasn't exactly at the top of her agenda. Sean did his best to help along with the spasmodic conversation, but there is a difficulty in entertaining a genuine A-list celebrity, if you have no idea who they are or what they do. Even worse, if, as in Sean's case, you do but your hosts don't and you can't believe they don't. There is a serious risk of embarrassment along the lines of asking the prime minister what he does for a living.

I imagine nowadays, or even fifteen years ago, one would have taken a hasty trawl through Wikipedia, as indeed I have just done, and been able to insert remarks like, "Are you concentrating on film work at present?" which would have got us through some of the conversational shoals. As it was, it was heavy going, hardly tempered by my apprehension that she might die at any moment. She looked ill enough.

I had also overestimated her age by twenty years.

Lunch eventually came to an end and we installed Nico in our front room and went rather nervously about our business.

I was on edge because she was chain smoking; I could quite see the need for it, but was not convinced she could carry on without setting fire to the sofa. Nothing much changed during the rest of the day and she was still on the sofa when I left for work on Monday.

There is an old story of two Victorian ladies emerging from seeing Sarah Bernhardt as Cleopatra. She had screamed, shouted, torn at the furnishings and finally killed herself, and one lady was heard saying to the other, "How different from the home life of our own dear queen." I felt a bit like that about Nico.

Though I had discovered she was quite famous (there are still fans of hers around today), I didn't feel any inclination to find out why, or even to listen to her music. Her lifestyle was so completely alien to ours. Some research on the internet since then hasn't made me feel very differently, though I have enjoyed some of the 'Velvet Underground' songs. She had a very beautiful voice.

Her connection with Andy Warhol and 'The Velvet Underground' had ceased twelve years before and in the interval she had acquired a serious heroin habit. She had appeared as herself in a small part in Fellini's 'La Dolce Vita'- I suppose I should have remembered this – and a number of other films which I probably should have seen and hadn't. By the time Nico came our way, she only had eight or nine years to live, though there was time for a successful come-back concert in New York and some sold-out American tours; also some heavy involvement in punk rock. I struggle to bridge the gap between the glamorous creature with the golden voice shown on her publicity stills and the incoherent wreck who sat at our dinner table.

By the time I got back on Monday evening, Nico had gone; she had left for Manchester with help from Sean. A couple of days later, Susan saw her being interviewed on BBC for a culture programme; she was much impressed by the interviewer's skill in conversing with her, although he did have the advantage of knowing what they were talking about.

The other day Ian, who comes to look after my garden in Cornwall, was having a sandwich with me. At sixty, I wondered if he was the right age to remember Nico. He thought a bit and a faraway look came into his eyes, "Velvet Underground," he said , "and to think you actually spoke to her."

Another memory from the 'end' of our time at Queen's Road was when Susan and I went off on our own, on holiday to Kashmir, leaving the young ones - our three, Sean, Cathy and her boyfriend, to hold the fort.

Probably this was one of the last times it was possible to visit Kashmir. It was timed for the end of July, right in the middle of the monsoon but equally the first time the passes became open after the winter snow. The programme was for us to fly to Delhi then take an internal flight to Srinagar, stay two or three days on a houseboat on the Dal Lake and then make for the mountains.

Srinagar was nothing very special but the Dal Lake was incredible. At the Srinagar end there were a string of houseboats, all built of wood according to a design which had probably been established for at least a hundred years. They were comfortable and elegant. Their drains fed straight into the lake.

Despite this, the lake remained serene and beautiful. The bird life was wonderful with an endless supply of pied kingfishers, hovering about fifteen feet up, and then suddenly diving. The lake was covered in lotus flowers and there was a floating island with a village on it where they had a market. I think it was one of the most beautiful places I have ever been – though you didn't want to go swimming in it.

There was one curious incident. During our time in Srinagar we visited some of the Moghul gardens. On the way into one – was it the Shalimar? -our tour guide Didi suddenly disappeared briefly. The explanation was that she had to speak to and pay an old witch camped at the gate. "On the last trip she definitely put the evil eye on us and we had the most appalling weather." Didi was absolutely not a push-over; and we certainly had excellent weather.

We went up to the foothills to acclimatise to the height and to meet our shikar. He was the head man and owner of the business. There were eight in our party, seven tourists plus Didi the tour guide. The shikar party was larger than this, as all the tents and food, some of it live, had to be transported on donkeys and mules. In addition, there was some valuable silver which had to be kept secure. There had to be enough hands to assemble the mess tent, plus all the accommodation tents, every afternoon and take it all down in the morning.

The silver was interesting. Our shikar's great-grandfather had performed the same function for the British Governor, who, when he retired, left him his houseboat with all its contents, including a large amount of silver and china. Sometime in the next hundred years there had been a disaster when the houseboat had capsized. The china had mostly been broken but the silver was recovered. So every evening, we dined off Victorian silver plates and dishes in our tent.

We had a number of chickens and ducks who travelled with us in wicker cages on top of the donkeys. In camp they were free range but always hung around the cooking tent, showing a considerable lack of perspicacity. The two cooks were both youngsters who performed amazing feats on open wood fires. Their final triumph on the last night was roast lamb (they had bought it from one of the herdsmen who were up in the mountains) followed by a spun sugar basket of crystallised sugar filled with fruit. The trip put a new slant on dressing for dinner. During the day it was shorts and a tee shirt; at six o'clock the sun went down and it was time to dress; pyjamas first followed by every available piece of clothing.

Susan playing a game of dice in Kashmir

Among the party were a Dutch vet and his wife. They had obviously done a lot of mountain walking and preferred not to ride. This must have been a bit tougher than he was used to and he succumbed to altitude sickness. We had two doctors in the party as well as two vets and they couldn't wait to treat him with diuretics. After one night standing outside in the Himalayan cold, he announced he didn't care if he died. That was the end of the treatment.

The surprising thing was quite how crowded the mountains were. We were travelling generally at about six thousand feet with occasional excursions up to ten thousand but we were in amongst herds of animals driven up to take advantage of the spring grass. We were riding on pony stallions, small and tough, which at the start of the ride were quite emaciated but gradually fattened up on the new grass.

One day when we weren't trekking, Susan and I managed to persuade the owners to let us take the ponies out for a hack. It was extraordinary, like riding on the Sussex downs, with the addition of some substantial mountains in the distance. We didn't stay out very long, but by the time we got back, panic had set in; the ponies were, I believe, worth about eighty pounds each and represented considerable wealth to the owners. However, no harm was done and everyone calmed down.

The head guy was a Hindu and his assistant (and best friend) was a Muslim. They worked together in harmony. I had a suspicion they were politically motivated in the cause of independence for Kashmir. If so, the last thirty years must have been totally devastating for them.

I mentioned that it was in the middle of the monsoon. We were incredibly lucky; this was one of the years when it didn't reach Kashmir. On top of this, the flowers were wonderful. We had had a brief taste of pre-monsoon weather. When we arrived in Delhi at one o'clock in the morning, the temperature was 38 Celsius.

Back in Kingston, there had been only one excitement. Our front bedroom had a door which swung shut of its own accord. It was a gift for Wellie, our springer spaniel. Normally, it was carefully kept shut but this time it had been left ajar; he had nosed his way in, watched everyone leaving in turn, until finally Emma left and in despair (he couldn't open the door) had leapt out of the window. There was a sloping roof underneath which slowed him up, but it was still quite a thump. Em took him to the vet who reckoned he was undamaged and as usual prescribed antibiotics.

Oh and there had been a party.

CHAPTER 20

Epilogue

I realise that I have now reached a point in my story where my children are likely to remember the course of events far more accurately than I am. So it's time to go back a bit, especially as not everyone who engages in writing this sort of memoir has the advantage of access to a substantial book written by his great-grandfather.

This one is called 'The Reminiscences of an Irish Land Agent' and my great grandfather was quite an important figure, at least in South West Ireland, since he acted as Land Agent i.e. manager, for some of the biggest, possibly even the majority of estates in the area. Because of this, a large part of his book is taken up with the difficulty of making a living out of farming in Ireland in the second half of the nineteenth century and the troubles and violence which sprang from it. So there is a lot of space devoted to Land Acts, Land Commissions and the like, things not much to my purpose.

What it also does, is give a very good flavour of what life was like in Ireland at the time and for that I am duly grateful. However to approach it at a slant:

My two grandmothers were both English, or as English as can generally be achieved; of my two grandfathers, one was pure Irish and one was pure Welsh; I have always felt much more attracted to the Irish side of the family than the Welsh, although I suppose I have felt English most of the time. Of course, the fact that both my grandfathers had died well before I was born, meant that they had no direct influence on my upbringing, whereas my grandmothers both lived on into my twenties. They weren't on speaking terms with each other, but this did not mean they pulled in different directions and they were both formidable characters.

As it happened, their lives were similar in that they had both at one time been relatively wealthy and finished up relatively poor. My father's mother, Granny, was a fairly straightforward case. She had inherited a substantial amount of money, presumably from her connection with the Meux brewery, made a disastrous marriage, acquired some expensive habits - apart from betting on and owning race horses, she was a dedicated socialite - there was talk of her having rented a house in Park Lane for 'the Season' - and many years later, she had been left, with the money running out, as a single parent supporting her younger son.

Gingie, my mother's mother, inherited several properties in the City of London, a property in Milk Street adjoining Cheapside for example, and was a wealthy woman. Her property was almost entirely destroyed in the Blitz and with it her income; she spent the war years living with my parents. By the time of her death in the fifties, there was still no sign of the property boom which fuelled developers like Clore and Samuel, and her estate was sold up fairly disastrously.

My Irish ancestors were certainly a lot more fun than the rest. As well as portraits, they left physical reminders of their existence. At the front of my great grandfather's published memoir, there is a photograph of him towards the end of his life. As a young man, he had been kicked in the face by a horse, re-arranging his nose fairly thoroughly, and this combined with his beard makes him resemble one of the (rather fanciful) portraits of Socrates.

We also inherited a fair amount of silverware, including, for a time, the Punchestown cup. This was a large silver-gilt wine-cooler, which when I was young, sat on the sideboard in my parents dining room. It had been made by Paul Storr, one of the greatest English silversmiths, but ruined as far as collectors of silver were concerned by the 'out of period' inscription, put on about seventy years after the cup had been made, to record my grandfather's riding his own horse, Lord Hugh, to win 'The Punchestown Cup.'

At the time, this was the top steeplechase for amateurs in Ireland. To ride in it and win was a considerable feat, as recognised by the quality of the trophy. As a child, I was greatly impressed by it and was even more impressed later on, when I had started riding myself and, incidentally, collecting silver, when I came to understand more about what it represented. And of course there had been a plot to shoot my grandfather on the way home from the event. It was certainly a handsome trophy which eventually succumbed to one of my parents' periods of acute insolvency.

The fact that it disappeared may have been symptomatic of the fact that my parents both regarded these aspirations to Irish blood and breeding as rather foolish. My mother of course, came from the Welsh side of the family, so there was no reason for her to be sympathetic to them. Even my father did nothing to encourage them; amused neutrality was his attitude. At the age of seventeen what counted for me was that I bore the same name as these men who had lived active and dangerous lives and at that time I was their sole male heir.

At some point a few years after the war, my father agreed to buy by subscription a family tree being prepared by one of his cousins. It is an impressive document on three scrolls of parchment although I don't think my father was much impressed. He couldn't very well get out of buying it, but thirty pounds was a lot of money in those days. I don't think it was really his scene. Apart from anything else, the mere fact of studying and taking interest in it seemed to imply a belief in inheritance which conflicted with his Socialist principles.

The author is not named on the parchments; I am not sure my father ever told me who had produced it as he was always rather tight lipped about it, but at the top, it refers to a load of papers left by my great aunt Charlotte, one of my great-grandfather Samuel Murray Hussey's daughters, who died in 1956 aged 92.There is a warning at the top that while all the official documents are accurately recorded, there is some 'deduction' (guesswork) used in linking names together.

Mention of Charlotte reminds me that the women of the family survived much better than the men. There were two of Samuel Murray's daughters still alive at the beginning of the second world war, including great aunt Dolly, who had been 'Keeper of the Holy Places' in Jerusalem and was reputed to swear in Arabic in her sleep. She was eventually removed from Jerusalem by the Foreign Office with some degree of compulsion. Her outspoken view on Arab/Israeli disagreements made her something of a loose cannon.

Returning to the family tree, it deals mainly with four family groups; the Blennerhassets, Fitzgeralds, Hicksons and Husseys, the last three being very closely linked as they went on marrying each other throughout the eighteenth and nineteenth centuries. Confusingly, they used a very narrow range of Christian names. The Hussey part of the tree is well enough documented, back to a Walter Hussey who was blown up by Cromwell in 1650. By the late eighteenth century it becomes quite detailed.

I have a portrait of my great great-grandfather Peter Bodkin Hussey hanging above me as I write. To judge by his clothing and his age it must have been painted about the time of his marriage in 1805; there was another link with him. I used to own a lozenge-shaped seal made of rock crystal, cut with three facets and engraved with the family coat of arms, the family crest (a hart under a tree) and the picture in profile of an unidentified man on the third side, presumably added for a bit of local colour. There is also a letter from Samuel Murray describing the seal and saying that it was cut from rock crystal found on the Blasquet Isles which were owned by his father. The seal was stolen in a burglary at our house in Kingston in 1987; I still have the letter, which now seems rather forlorn.

The earliest artefacts, which can be identified as belonging to the family, and which we still own, are three silver spoons made in Dublin dating back to around 1704 with a rather primitive contemporary version of the family crest on them. They are a pattern known as rat-tail which is typical of Dublin silver.

Judging from the parchments, the family goes back to the seventeenth century. With a bit of imagination one can believe it went back far earlier, though there is an increasing number of 'Probable' identifications. There had been times when it had looked as though the name would die out, most recently in the period when the only surviving male Husseys were my father and his brother, both unmarried at that time and neither at all well.

We have gone beyond that now. As far as I know there is no one still alive, apart from my immediate family, from the Southern Irish branch with the Hussey name. I have seven grandchildren and the four boys, apart from a suicidal tendency to indulge in extreme sports, are all notably fit and well, but none of them is called Hussey.

It looks as though that's the end of it, at least as far as the branch from the South West of Ireland is concerned, but by an unlikely coincidence, a friend of Susan's married someone called John Hussey, a farmer in Wiltshire. He and I compared notes, and as far as we could tell we were not related, but did share the same family crest including the motto 'Cor Immobile' (in English 'Steadfast Heart'). So there will be some English Husseys around for a bit.

The solution to the problem of finding male heirs was partially solved in the nineteenth century by having enormous families; Peter Bodkin had eleven children and Samuel Murray had ten, but the mortality rate particularly among the males, both children and adults, was appalling. Samuel Murray was the only male to outlive his father; and my grandfather, Maurice Fitzgerald, was Samuel Murray's last remaining son and only survived his father by three years.

I wonder how much this question of the survival of the family name would have bothered them. The Husseys were so intermingled with the Hicksons and the Fitzgeralds that perhaps they didn't notice. Both Peter Bodkin and Samuel Murray married their first cousins, who were both Hicksons, two of Samuel Murray's daughters married Fitzgeralds and my grandfather's middle name was Fitzgerald. Perhaps they looked on the family as an assembly of all three families, all living in the same region of Ireland. And that of course all changed when my father and uncle were brought over to England, as children, by their mother. So perhaps my father was right and all this interest in the Irish connection was merely foolishness if the family were no longer living in Ireland.

My father converted to Catholicism. Prior to that, the family had all been brought up as protestants and this went right back to Peter Bodkin Hussey. Before that they were Catholic. Peter Bodkin was known as 'Red Precipitate' on account of his red hair and his quick temper; the story in the family was that he had had to leave the church on account of having floored the parish priest in the course of a dispute. The truth was more prosaic, as is made clear in Samuel Murray's book, it was simply part of Peter Bodkin's parents' marriage settlement that his mother, who was protestant, was in charge of the children's education. Not that the settlement itself didn't cause quite an uproar.

Samuel Murray was at times seriously at odds with the local catholic clergy. Here he is quoting a parish priest, preaching on the evils of drink, "It's whisky makes you bate your wives; it's whisky makes your homes desolate; it's whisky makes you shoot your landlords, and" – with emphasis as he thumped the pulpit – "it's whisky that makes you miss them." Samuel Murray then adds, "There is as much truth in that sermon as in any that was preached last Sunday between Belfast and Glengariff." Perhaps not precisely the endorsement the clergy would be looking for.

There is a story in his memoir which illustrates his relations with the tenants. A tenant had died and his son came to have the tenancy agreement, including a rent of £25 a year, transferred to him. Having checked that he was his father's sole heir, Samuel Murray asked, "What will become of your brother and sister?" "Oh, they will get what I draw". (That was the money that, when he married, his wife would bring as dowry) "What will happen if that's quite little, say £20?" "Oh, that would never do at all, I have been rated at £160." In the upshot, my great grandfather discovered that he had got £170, so it ended happily.

South West Ireland at various times in the nineteenth century must have resembled the 'Wild West' of America. Someone who had been to a dance at Edenburn, Samuel Murray's house near Castleisland, in the eighteen seventies recalled that so many pistols had been brought by the guests that the room assigned for 'hats and coats' wasn't big enough and they had to be put in the smoking room.

Edenburn itself was blown up in 1884, or at least the back of it was. There were sixteen people in the house, including two policemen but no one was hurt except the butler who was hit by falling plaster. "Dynamite's like an Irishman's pig," said my great grandfather, "you point it one way and it goes another." With that he went back to bed.

There was no doubt of the intention to kill the whole household; the explosion was heard four miles away in Castleisland. My great grandfather attributed the attack to the

Irish Land League; certainly they were the most active political group in the area. Although officially they discouraged violence, threats from them had been taken sufficiently seriously that Sunday afternoons were given over to pistol practice at Edenburn.

According to Samuel Murray they refused to pay the agreed fee for the atrocity, as no one had been killed, which resulted in the leading bomber taking a pot shot at the treasurer of the Castleisland Branch of the Land League. There had been a suggestion that the tenants, who lived in the vicinity of Edenburn, must have been involved. As a body they wrote to the local paper to deny this most emphatically.

As well as the attacks on Samuel Murray, there were also several attempts on my grandfather Maurice Fitzgerald Hussey's life. As mentioned earlier, he was nicknamed 'Snipe' owing to the difficulty of shooting him. In Charlestown, County Mayo an innocent man was mistaken for him, (he was sheltering from the rain under an umbrella) and died of the injuries he received in the attack. Somewhat improbably, there was an attempt to ambush my grandfather on the way home from the races by building a wall across the road he was expected to take in his pony and trap. It didn't succeed.

Eventually his house at Aghadoe, overlooking the lakes at Killarney, was burnt down by Sinn Fein, but that was after his death and may have been an accident. I visited it in 1985 when it had been rebuilt and was being run as a youth hostel. I believe it has now been rebuilt as a hotel.

Despite all this, both my grandfather and his father managed to live fairly ordinary and extremely busy lives, making long daily journeys by train or pony and trap. Of course they carried a pair of loaded pistols which they kept beside them always. And they sometimes had police protection as well.

Officially, they were two of the most hated men in Ireland but there was another side to the coin. For example; a Dutchman called Harenc had died, leaving an enormous estate of 60875 acres in north Kerry. Needless to say there had been a lot of manoeuvring between the various parties involved in the inheritance and these eventually resolved into cases in court. Eventually, a group of fifty of the tenants, who wished to protect their interests, including the right to buy their holdings, came together and asked Samuel Murray to purchase the estate on their behalf. The price he offered was considerable, £80,000 (equivalent to £4 million today). There is no means of telling where the money came from; he speaks as though it had been his personal cash but, if it belonged to other people, at the least it argues a considerable degree of trust in his abilities.

He was successful in buying the estate and the news was greeted with considerable rejoicing; bonfires were lit in Castleisland and Tralee and general merrymaking ensued. Sometime afterwards, Samuel Murray stood for election in Tralee and his opponents tried to use the Harenc affair to blackguard him. The tenants were so outraged that they got together and published a defence of his behaviour as a landlord.

Later, under the new Land Acts, the land was compulsorily purchased by the same government who had sold it to him, at a discount of roughly a third. Not unnaturally, he was extremely aggrieved.

Both Samuel Murray and his eldest son were JPs and both had been High Sheriff of Kerry. As agent for some of the largest estates in Kerry, Samuel Murray was required to give evidence before several commissions. We only have his version of what was said and how he performed as a witness, but he could hardly have put forward an outrageously misleading version in the lifetime of the other participants. From his account he appears to have acquitted himself well.

When Samuel Murray died in his bed, at the age of eighty-nine, three hundred people attended the funeral. As he would have said, that was probably just to see him safely buried, although perhaps it also meant he wasn't hated quite as much as his enemies would have had us believe.

He died more than a hundred years ago and the circumstances of his life could hardly have been more different from mine, yet I feel from reading his book as though I had known him well, not just as a friend but as a close relation. He was held in high esteem as a wit and teller of stories and these ghosted reminiscences hardly do him justice. There is an apology at the beginning for their colloquialism, I think stiffness would have been a more reasonable complaint. When I first read his book as a youngster I was quite dismissive of it. Now I feel differently. There is nothing like trying to do something oneself to learn how difficult it is. And I've certainly enjoyed his stories.

Perhaps one of these would do to finish with; A senior barrister, Philip O'Connell had advised his client – called Flaherty – that his action (over a debt) would turn on whether the defendant had admitted the debt to a witness within the last six years. That, without any delay, he absolutely had to find a man to swear to this. O'Connell had then gone off to chair a dinner given for a new county court judge. In my great grandfather's words: "As the dessert was being laid on the table there was a loud knock on the door which was just behind the chairman. 'What is it?' cried O'Connell. A head appeared and a voice from it explained:

"I'm Tim Flaherty, your honour, as was consulting you outside, and I want you to come this way for a while."

"Don't you see I'm engaged and cannot come?"

"But it's pressing and important!"

"I tell you I won't come!"

Then at the top of his voice, Tim yells,"Will a small woman do as well your honour?'